GARDEN-
INSPIRED
QUILTS

DESIGN JOURNALS FOR 12 QUILT PROJECTS

Jean & Valori Wells

PHOTOGRAPHY BY VALORI WELLS

C&T PUBLISHING

©2002 Jean Wells and Valori Wells

Editor: Candie Frankel
Technical Editor: Carolyn Aune
Copy Editor: Stacy Chamness
Photographer: Valori Wells
Cover Designer: Christina D. Jarumay
Design Director/Book Designer: Christina D. Jarumay
Illustrator: Kirstie McCormick
Production Assistants: Tim Manibusan, Kirstie McCormick

Front cover: Quilted zinnia by Jean Wells; zinnia photograph by Valori Wells

Back cover: *Summer Celebration* by Jean Wells; portion of *Solitude* by Valori Wells; photographs by Valori Wells

Published by C&T Publishing, Inc., P.O. Box 1456, Lafayette, Ca. 94549

Attention Teachers: C&T Publishing, Inc., encourages you to use this book as a text for teaching. Contact us at 800-284-1114 or www.ctpub.com for more information about the C&T Teachers Program.

Library of Congress Cataloging-in-Publication Data
Wells, Jean.
  Garden-inspired quilts:design journals for 12 quilt projects/Jean and Valori Wells.
     p. cm.
  ISBN 1-57120-131-9
  1. Quilting–Patterns. 2. Gardens in art. 3. Photography of gardens.
I. Wells, Valori. II. Title.
  TT835 .W4653 2002
  746.46'041–dc21
                            2001006146

Printed in China
10 9 8 7 6 5 4 3 2 1

Dedication

To John Keenan, husband and stepfather,
who is always encouraging and supportive
of all our creative endeavors.

Acknowledgments

Visiting other people's gardens is like stepping into their private worlds. You learn about gardeners through their selection of plants and the arrangement of plants in the garden. We would like to thank the following people who so graciously welcomed us into their gardens: Maggie and Jason, Larry and Jeff, Mary, Sally, Anne, and Bunnies By The Bay.

The Stitchin' Post staff is very helpful to us during times of deadlines, and we appreciate them greatly. Patricia Raymond was invaluable as a quilter, as were stitchers Gerri Moore and Barbara Ferguson.

Christina Jarumay designed our last three books, and we love how she combines the photographs and text to convey the essence of what we have been trying to capture all along. Her sense of color in the design is wonderful. She is the final link in helping us to fulfill our vision of bringing photographs and quilts together in a way that is inspiring and beautiful to our readers.

It was a pleasure to work again with Candie Frankel as an editor. Her attention to the flow of the text helps us to get our point across. Her talents are invaluable. We were also fortunate to work once again with technical editor Carolyn Aune, who checks and double-checks all the how-to details.

Todd Hensley and the C&T family have believed in our projects from the beginning. We appreciate the opportunity they have given us to create inspirational how-to books for quilters.

Table of

Contents

Preface

Watching people discover their creative potential and accomplish their goals is very satisfying to us. We wrote this book to share the discovery process and quilting techniques we've followed to create one-of-a-kind quilts inspired by the garden. We find the garden holds a wealth of information for anyone interested in color and design. Maybe we can open your eyes to possibilities that would be perfect in your next quilt. The journal approach taken in the text will, we hope, encourage you along your own journey of discovery.

Jean's garden is a living palette of inspiration waiting to be interpreted. Gardens everywhere—even the one in your own backyard—offer the same opportunity for personal, innovative quiltmaking. Let us show you where to begin.

Inspiration

Where do ideas come from?

Everything around us influences the way we create. Even when we think we aren't paying attention, shapes, designs, and colors are continuously working their way into our memories. One of the ways to access these hidden influences is to make a conscious effort to see what is around us—to become more observant.

Perhaps you pass by a particular tree every day on your way to work without really paying much attention to it. Pause and take a closer look at the way it is structured. How do the branches unfold? What colors do you see? How do the colors change with the seasons, or from hour to hour? This exercise doesn't mean you're going to go home and make a tree quilt. It does mean that you'll know what to look for when a subject that does interest you comes along.

Perhaps you grow poppies in your garden. Think about all of the stages the plants go through, from bud to flower and finally to seed pod. You may want to keep a photographic record of these stages and use them someday in a quilt. But even casual observations become automatically stored in our memory banks and can be drawn on for future use.

It is inevitable that some days you will be a more receptive observer than others. When rushed or preoccupied with daily tasks, we naturally see less. Allow yourself time to observe and gather ideas for future quilts. A quiet bench in the park or your own garden can become a spot to contemplate and dream in a relaxed setting. Seating in the garden is an invitation to slow down and become part of nature. Seats capture the walker. When you sit down, you contemplate and study the garden from a different perspective than you do while walking. Taking time to reflect on what you see will open your mind to possibilities for design and color while fulfilling your creative longings.

Consider keeping a quilt design journal for the ideas that you collect. Your ideas might take the form of a simple sketch, a written description, or a photograph that you glue in. Maybe you buy some fabulous fabric but are not sure what you want to do with it. Paste a swatch in your notebook. One day an idea will click and you will be off and running. In *Garden-Inspired Quilts*, a journal entry accompanies each project to show how ideas and images collected over time eventually coalesce.

Daily life in the garden is never dull, as there are always new things to look at. The first daffodils of spring are so uplifting, perhaps because we know they have fought their way through snow and a cold winter to emerge. Maybe it is their sunny yellow color or the bell shape of the flowers that makes them appear so cheerful. For some people, daffodils symbolize the fresh breath of spring after the winter. For others, they announce the beginning of warmer weather and a new garden season. The different shades of yellow might inspire a palette.

contemplate and dream

Be curious. Train yourself to be an observer. Look at the underside of a flower and examine the design lines and colors lurking there. You might be surprised at the combinations you find. Think about the curiosity you had as a child. Back then, if you wanted to know about something, you moved in for a closer look, touching, sometimes tasting, to find out more.

Don't be afraid to get down on your hands and knees and take a look at a flower from the ground or to climb up on a bench and look down on it. A poppy viewed from the side presents a different shape than when viewed from above. Valori always takes several shots of a flower from different angles. Later on, she has a ready reference for shapes, lines, and colors.

be an observer

Develop an eye for the proportions of the colors in nature's compositions. If a flower or particular spot in the garden is pleasing to you, jot down your observations. What percentage of the composition is true orange, deeper orange, medium green, softer green, and so forth? Study your notes at a later date and apply the same principles to one of your quilt compositions. This technique can be used in any quilting palette situation.

Colors continually influence us, and our response to them can be positive, negative, or anywhere in between. Some people are comfortable with soft, muted colors, others like clear, bright vibrant hues, and still others prefer earthy neutrals. Our color perceptions change with the setting. Go outside at dusk or early in the morning to experience a different mood in your garden. Note how the evening and early morning light make purple and lavender shades appear more concentrated and intense. Stroll through the garden on a foggy day or during a light spring rain and soak in the muted color impressions you receive.

be curious

Gardening and garden photography have opened up a whole new world of color to the two of us. Being aware of the color in our everyday surroundings has made us more adventuresome in our color choices for quilting. For example, seeing orange flowers in the garden gave Jean the courage to use some orange fabric in her quilt *Summer Celebration*. The proportion rule works well here— a little orange goes a long way. Similarly, the palette for *Paradise in the Garden* did not materialize on its own. Bit by bit, the exuberant colors in this quilt found their way into Jean's creative mind. By working in the flower beds daily and tossing freshly cut flowers in a basket, she was able to see these many different colors displayed together.

Another valuable color insight is the role green plays in nature. Green truly is Mother Nature's neutral. For any given color, there is some shade of green that will work with it. In Anne Sutton's garden, the green foundation is ivy, and Anne and her husband have trained it to grow in topiaries as well as garlands along the edges of the flower boxes. We become Mother Nature's helpers in the garden. No where is this more evident than in a city rooftop garden like that of Larry Ruhl. His garden was created with pots and planter boxes. When you consider that all that soil had to be carried to the rooftop and a watering system had to be devised, you recognize this lush, green garden for the labor of love it is.

Green is Mother

When you are planting a garden, you have a certain amount of control over the palette. Jean laid out her vegetable patch so that the colors of the ripened produce would create a medallion-style block. Being Jean, she couldn't resist tucking in a few zinnias and putting marigolds at the corners. As the vegetables matured, she couldn't bear to harvest them and leave a hole in the design. You may wonder if at this point she was creating a garden or a quilt. But in fact, the two go hand in hand, each one influencing and drawing inspiration from the other.

Nature's neutral

Gardeners often display architectural pieces and collectibles among their plantings. These might include trellises and other structural supports, chairs and benches for seating, and purely decorative items such as gazing balls and statuary. Garden ornaments like these can also inspire a quilt design. In *Meadow Medallion*, the focus of the design—an antique metal grille—first appeared in a garden setting.

Water is another element that can enrich the garden setting and encourage mental reflection. Water can be introduced in a birdbath or simple bowl, a fountain, a pond, a creek, or a waterfall. When Jean built her creek and waterfall, she was immediately taken with the sounds of the water going over, under, and around rocks. She realized that she could change the sound by moving the rocks around. Sitting beside the creek at lunchtime gives her a break from the busy workday. The sound of running water is very calming and encourages meditation and reflection. It can also stir up ideas and help you find solutions to design dilemmas.

Creativity is a personal, reflective experience.

Other garden ornaments are less predictable. Like fabric in a quilt, they can spur the imagination in one direction or another. Improvisational art, like filling a wheelbarrow with plants, adds unexpected interest, and you'll find yourself taking a second look, just as we did at Bunnies By The Bay in La Conner, Washington. The whirligigs atop the fence are made from ordinary household objects. An old washboard, a rocking horse, and interesting pieces of wood appear on the fence and among the garden plantings. Objects like these arouse curiosity and invite speculation about their presence. Anne Sutton does something similar in her quilt *Garden Sweet Garden*. At first glance, the quilt appears conventional enough, but then your eye gravitates toward the garden scene in the center of each block. After viewing one scene, you want to take in another and another.

Many a student walks into one of our "garden-inspired quilting" classes a little frantic or insecure about taking a new approach to quilt design. We find that the garden provides beautiful, familiar subject matter for helping them cross that bridge. Being creative and coming up with a unique quilt design is not a complex process. By working with a favorite flower or leaf, a student gains confidence in her ability to collect information about color and shape that will prove valuable to her as a quilter.

Drawing inspiration from the garden is a personal undertaking, one that involves your own unique perspective. It can be as simple as putting the beautiful colors from your grandmother's flower garden into a traditional block quilt. Memories of her garden will come flooding back to you every time you view the quilt. The excitement that you experience along the way as you strive to capture the

essence of something close to you is part of the enjoyment. Other people are bound to come away with different impressions when viewing your finished quilt, a sign of just how personal creative inspiration really is.

Interpretation

How do I put my ideas to work?

In this book, we will take you through the design process for twelve different quilts. You will become acquainted with the trials and tribulations we faced as we moved from inspiration to interpretation to finished quilt.

Decision making is an integral part of the design process, and we will give you the tools you need to work out your own solutions to the design dilemmas you encounter along the way. Refer to your favorite quilting book for instructions on rotary cutting, piecing, and quilting, because we won't be covering those basics here. Instead, our goal is to help you understand how each quilt came to be. Interpreting an original idea for a quilt can be a challenge when you haven't done it before. A simple way to start is to work a traditional pattern in a color palette drawn from your garden experience. Valori took this approach for *Log Cabin City Garden*. When the block construction is already familiar, you can concentrate your efforts on fabric and color choices. Too many challenges can cause you to lose your creative energy. We don't want that!

Maybe you are ready for a little bit bigger challenge. *Meadow Medallion* combines several quilting techniques. The meadow theme in the background fabric is developed with a watercolor piecing technique. The actual piecing is easy, but the fabric choices and their placement in the diagonal grid require careful planning. Your garden photographs are an invaluable reference in developing a background layer like this.

More technically challenging quilts will obviously require more thinking and design time. Usually, your first step is to decide what sewing technique is the most appropriate to carry out your idea. Will the quilt be appliquéd or foundation-pieced? Will the seam lines be straight or curved? Once you nail down the construction methods, you can focus on quilt size and fabric type and color.

You may have a wall- or bed-size quilt in mind, but try to be flexible and let the design itself suggest an appropriate size and shape to you. You can change the quilt dimensions up to the very end, as Sally Frey discovered with *Kenmar Farm Baskets*. Would an intimate setting work well for your chosen subject matter, or do the different elements in your design need more space to float in? Keep your options open by folding the excess fabric under, rather than cutting it off, until you are sure.

Fabric plays an obvious role in a quilt design, and it's important to choose fabrics that match the style and mood of the quilt. In *Kenmar Farm Baskets*, busy little prints alongside the plaids would leave you dizzy, but batik-style fabrics worked perfectly. Similarly, contemporary fabrics would look out of place with the whimsical mood Anne Sutton created in *Garden Friends*. Color is another fabric feature to consider. When Valori photographs a single flower up close, the background often becomes a soft, shapeless blur of color. There are lots of color clues here. Each quilt journal explains how the particular color choices for that quilt were made.

Borders pose challenges to quilters and gardeners alike. A successful border, whether it be rocks along a garden path or a two-inch-wide strip of fabric around the edge of a quilt, defines a line that the eye can follow. Is a border even needed? When we begin our quilts, we may think we know the answer, but sometimes as the quilt nears completion, it tells us otherwise. The quilt journals describe how border decisions are made as well.

For the details in your design, look directly to nature. You already know how to observe a leaf or flower, take notes and close-up reference photographs, and make a simple sketch. Now you need to figure out how to convey those details using fabric and thread. Leaf veins, for instance, can be satin-stitched by machine or cut from contrasting fabric and fused in place. Hand-embroidery can also be used.

The final layering and quilting gives you yet another opportunity to express the details. By repeating the shapes from your quilt top in your quilting design, you unify the entire quilt in a subtle way. We love this part of quilting, and Valori really shines in this area. When she seriously took up quilting, she figured you could stitch whatever design you liked. With limited knowledge and experience, she dove in and learned to free-motion quilt, taking her design ideas from nature. Valori taught Jean how to free-motion quilt, and now she too does all of her own design work and has gained confidence in the stitching.

To make a garden quilt, you have to move forward from inspiration to interpretation. This means taking the visual clues the garden gives you and figuring out how to express them using the familiar elements of quilting—shape, line, color, texture, stitching, and embellishment. But there is another element. A garden is a bit like a dream, and you want to capture its overall mood, too. Pulling all the elements together into a single visual harmony is what quilting—and gardening—is all about.

Log Cabin City Garden

BY VALORI WELLS

Larry Ruhl is a good friend of the family who lives in New York City. He works in the fabric industry and has collected antique quilts for fourteen years. More recently, Larry has been bitten by the gardening bug. For the past two years, he has been cultivating his new passion on a rooftop in the middle of Manhattan. I had been hearing about this rooftop garden and wanted to photograph it. In September of 2000, I went to visit Larry and Jeff and see their unique setting. I was fascinated by the idea of a garden in the middle of such a hectic city.

I arrived in New York and met them at the apartment building. We rode the elevator up to the twelfth floor. Once I was inside the apartment, the tall ceilings and large windows gave me the impression of being in a house. On the far end of the room near the windows a metal spiral staircase drew my eyes upward. We climbed up to a large door that opened like a hatch onto the small private garden space. Outside, a few steps led down to the garden floor. A table and chairs sat at the base of the steps, surrounded by the lush plant growth and tall wooden fencelike walls—a true sanctuary after a long day at the office.

The garden is about ten feet wide and forty feet long. The area behind the stairwell and door functions like a potting shed; this is where all the tools and necessities to keep the garden growing are kept. Larry does all of the planting and decorating, while Jeff attends to the technical aspects of the garden, including a drip irrigation system. This system is their savior, as the rooftop receives full sun throughout the day. Their watering method is all the more remarkable given that there aren't any traditional in-the-ground flower beds. All of the plants are potted, and different sizes and shapes of pots overflow with multiple plantings.

Larry has established a collection of perennials and fills in with hearty annuals every year. A large raspberry bush had been producing fruit all summer long. Pots full of vines—Boston and English ivies—grow up the wooden fence. Sage, oregano, mint, and lavender mix their herby scents with those of the flowers and greenery. If it weren't for the buildings jutting out of the skyline, I would think I was in someone's backyard.

Tucked among the pots and plants were various collectibles. Larry and Jeff are avid antique collectors, so it didn't surprise me that the garden was full of unique objects: rusted candlestick holders for a romantic dinner on the roof, old urns, washbasins, even antique sprinklers and garden tools, which Larry regularly uses.

One of the plantings is a ground cover with little purple flowers that Larry fell in love with. He likes the way it grows out of the pot and down the sides, filling the empty space and breaking up the color and shape of the containers. Another favorite is oriental grasses combined with a viney ground cover. Because I arrived in September, the spring and summer flowers weren't blooming, but their foliage remained and gave texture to the garden. I was reminded of how easy it is to miss seeing the foliage on a plant when the flower is in bloom.

In one corner, chalkware chickens and a painted cement gnome sat tucked among the foliage. A star rested on a table against the wood fence, the various aged woods playing their subtle textures off of one another. Seemingly oblivious of their conversation, a potted vine deftly wended its way into their space.

Hanging on one of the fence walls was a ceramic wreath of pansies, originally made as a tombstone decoration for a French cemetery. Larry and Jeff brought it back with them from Paris, and it seems to fit perfectly in their garden. On one garden wall, Larry hung one of his antique quilts, a beautiful old Log Cabin made from shirts, pants, ties, and other garments. I immediately fell in love with this quilt. The entire garden was so simple and beautiful, beyond what I had imagined.

For a different twist on the city garden, I visited my brother Jason and his wife Maggie in Portland, Oregon. Jason and Maggie live in a 1926 bungalow. The front yard is on an incline, rising from the sidewalk to the raised porch on either side of the front steps. The beds are full of different ground covers—woolly thyme, blue star creeper, roman chamomile, and sedum, to name a few. There is a blueberry bush, a Japanese maple, and a Japanese willow, along with some grasses that I couldn't identify. Ground covers grow around the rocks and over the edges, while passionflower, Montana clematis, and Tangerine Beauty crossvines wind their way up the posts and through the beams of the open-roofed porch.

The backyard has witnessed an amazing transformation since Jason and Maggie first moved in. Initially, the thirty-by-forty-foot yard was covered with grass and ended with a tall laurel hedge at the back. A few iris and dahlia plants were established, and the dahlias—with huge flower heads almost the size of the family cats—bloomed profusely from July through September. Jason and Maggie took out all of the grass and put a couple of raised beds against the fence, where they grow lettuce, sugar pot peas, Walla Walla onions, and horseradish, among other things.

At the opposite end of the garden, a slate path leads from a patio to a small waterfall and pond. The pond is full of water lettuce, lilies, and hyacinth, along with a couple of koi, which keep the cats entertained. At the top, the water flows over the rocks past two metal fish. Jason tells me that if you move the fish around, the sound of the water changes. Even though the fixture is small, the sound of the trickling water travels through the yard, making you forget you are in a city.

Jason and Maggie's neighbors grow grapes on their side of the fence, and some of the vines hang over, providing an extra treat. The fence has weathered to a subtle gray. I was very attracted by the colors of the vines and their fruit—the green of the new leaf growth compared with the turned-up rust and creamy edges of the dying leaves, the deep purple of the ripe grapes and the soft green of the unripe grapes. Nearby was a birdbath with similar hues.

Both of these city gardens were inspiring to me, but I didn't realize they would come together in my designing until I started going through my photographs. I kept coming back to Larry's Log Cabin quilt and all of the old "stuff" he's assembled in his garden. I wondered how I might infuse this classic quilt design with my own contemporary twist. I knew that simply reproducing the antique version wouldn't be interesting enough for me. As I was mulling this over, I turned to my dahlia and grape photos. Then it hit me: Why not make a Log Cabin quilt in the dahlia, grape, and fence colors?

I started with the Log Cabin design. I had only one photograph of the full quilt, but that was enough to let me examine its beautiful subtleties. The light fabrics were not only cream-colored but included notes of tan and soft gray. In the darks, there were the ranges of brown, reds, blues, and golds. The colors didn't appear in any particular sequence; it seemed to me that the quiltmaker just used them as they became available.

When I put the quilt photo next to the grape photos, I started visualizing how the palette would work. My light fabrics would be the soft green of the unripe grapes, the light gray of the fence, the creamy tan of the dying leaves, and soft rust. I found my darks lurking among the ripe grapes, the leaves, the vines, and the shadowed areas of the fence.

Now I had to find the fabrics. I chose to work with hand-dyed, hand-painted, and solid batik fabrics. I wanted to achieve the aura of the old Log Cabin but without using printed fabrics. Picking the fabrics for this quilt was a lot of fun. I found that I couldn't be too literal in choosing the colors or it would get boring, so I let my purples run to the blue side and let the rusts get a little orange. On the light side I played with the gray and soft peach, the green and purple so that there were subtle changes. The lighter colors offered less room for play than the dark, rich colors. For sparkle, I included a bit of rust in the darks and some light rust and green in the lights.

I laid out the blocks in the same setting as the antique quilt. My quilt ended up being bigger, which was fine with me, since I like to use my quilts. I machine-quilted grape leaves and vines as a way of tying in my original color inspiration. I wanted the quilting to blend in with the color changes, so I used light thread in the light areas and changed to darker thread for the dark areas.

The way that this design evolved is one of my favorite ways to quilt. I take a traditional block and work it up in colors that remind me of a favorite place. When I quilt this way, I can really focus on color.

Log Cabin City Garden

Pieced and quilted by Valori Wells; 75½" x 75½".

■ MATERIALS

Hand-dyed fabrics create the textural mood in this scrap quilt. Choose a wide variety of fabrics for the light and dark side of the center squares.

1/3 yard for center squares

3 3/4 yards assorted fabrics for light side

4 yards assorted fabrics for dark side

1/2 yard for binding

4 1/2 yards backing

80" x 80" batting

■ CUTTING

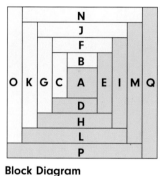

Block Diagram

The quilt contains 100 Log Cabin blocks. Follow the block diagram, cutting guide, and directions that follow to cut 1 center square and 16 pieces for each block. Sewing precut lengths encourages piecing accuracy and makes it easy to vary the color combinations from block to block.

CUTTING GUIDE			
Light		**Dark**	
		A	2" x 2"
B	1 1/4" x 2"	D	1 1/4" x 2 3/4"
C	1 1/4" x 2 3/4"	E	1 1/4" x 3 1/2"
F	1 1/4" x 3 1/2"	H	1 1/4" x 4 1/4"
G	1 1/4" x 4 1/4"	I	1 1/4" x 5"
J	1 1/4" x 5"	L	1 1/4" x 5 3/4"
K	1 1/4" x 5 3/4"	M	1 1/4" x 6 1/2"
N	1 1/4" x 6 1/2"	P	1 1/4" x 7 1/4"
O	1 1/4" x 7 1/4"	Q	1 1/4" x 8"

For the A center squares, cut five 2" x 42" strips; cut into 100 squares, each 2" x 2".

For the light side of the blocks, cut 100 strips, each 1 1/4" x 42". Following the cutting guide, cut 100 each of B, C, F, G, J, K, N, and O. I stacked several strips and cut the stack into different lengths to make sure the colors would not always appear in the same place in the block. Organize the pieces by their letter label.

For the dark side of the blocks, cut 108 strips, each 1 1/4" x 42". Following the cutting guide, cut 100 each of D, E, H, I, L, M, P, and Q.

■ INSTRUCTIONS

1. Place A and B right sides together. With B on top, stitch 1/4" from the edge. When you near the end of the seam, pick up another A and B, stack them, and feed them into the machine as you finish the first set. Repeat to make 100 units. Cut apart and press toward B.

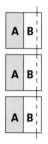

2. Pick up a C and place under AB, right sides together. Stitch as shown, chaining the units together as in step 1. Cut apart and press toward C.

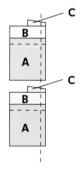

3. Stitch each D to an ABC as shown. Cut apart and press toward D.

4. Stitch each E to an ABCD as shown. Cut apart and press toward E.

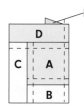

5. The first round is now complete. If you look at your blocks, you will see light pieces on two sides of the center square and dark pieces on the other two sides. Continue adding light and dark pieces in the established sequence. Make 100 blocks with four rounds each.

6. Arrange the blocks as shown in the quilt photo (page 29). Stitch the blocks together in rows. Press. Join the rows. Press.

7. Layer and finish the quilt.

Quilting Design
Enlarge to desired size

Garden Sweet Garden

BY ANNE SUTTON

Hearts have always been a favorite of mine. I have them all over my house and am always hunting for more to add to my collection. When my husband and I were landscaping our yard, we had no idea the heart theme would invade our garden as well. We were simply making improvements to our little house.

It started with a picture of a heart-shaped lawn that I saw in a garden book. I asked my husband if he might duplicate it in our backyard. Since grass doesn't grow well in the shade of the big trees, he suggested building a heart-shaped planter instead. The planter was designed using broken pieces of cement recycled from the patio that we were tearing up.

Many other hearts can be discovered throughout our garden. Part of the fun is trying to spot them. A pyracantha, trained to grow in a heart shape, climbs on the back fence. Hearts appear in the topiaries I so enjoy creating. A heart-shaped stick supports a plant. Next year I am determined to add more "honey-do's" to my list—perhaps heart-shaped stepping stones to lead us down the garden path.

I knew when I started designing a quilt with a garden theme that it would have to include hearts. My idea was to have each block represent a scene or object in my garden. The background of the block would have to be large enough to accommodate these various appliqués. I chose the Shoo Fly block for its large middle square, knowing that the half-square triangles in the corners would add interest to the quilt. As I played with various sashing ideas, I liked the way narrow sashing coupled with wider sashing added a secondary smaller block to the set. If I appliquéd small hearts to these corner posts, I could tie all of the blocks together.

My color inspiration came from a fabric in Moda's "High Tea" collection by Sandy Gervais. All of the colors in the background blocks were pulled from this one fabric. The mood was soft and luscious, reminding me of old-fashioned ice cream flavors like raspberry, lemon, and lime. (After I chose the palette, I realized that the antique stove on my deck was the same lemony tone.)

To make the blocks stand out, I chose colors and prints in slightly deeper tones. The hearts use six different raspberry reds in the same value, so what gets noticed are the subtle changes in pattern. The green check in the corner posts, from a 1930s line of reproduction fabric, reminded me of a garden trellis. The appliqués inside the hearts use a variety of small-scale prints.

To find inspiration for the appliqué designs, I strolled around my garden with a notebook and pencil in hand. I sketched and made notes. We have lots of topiaries. A glance at our many birdhouses reminded me that several bunnies visit the garden every morning, waiting for us to throw birdseed on the ground. Mr. Max, the cat, can often be found lounging in the sun. And, of course, flowers, pots, and benches seem to pop up everywhere. Back in my studio, the hard part was choosing my twelve favorites.

A green garden bench was a must—all of the wooden benches in our garden are painted this signature color. I traced a bench directly from a photograph and worked from there to develop the appliqué design. When I end up with small, overlapping pieces, I first like to arrange them and fuse them to one another on an appliqué pressing sheet. Then I can fuse them as a unit to the quilt block. This technique helps me keep small pieces positioned in their proper places.

Two of the appliqué designs—the basket of flowers and the pot of tulips—were taken from an old booklet called *Old-Fashioned Quilts* by Carlie Sexton, printed in Wheaton, Illinois, in 1928. My friend Margaret Peters found it in an antique sewing box that her husband bought for her. The flower appliqués in the basket were my contribution.

I used machine and hand embroidery to add texture and color to many of the appliqués, working buttonhole stitch around the edges first and then fitting in other details. The bunny holds a lazy daisy stitch flower, Mr. Snail has a French knot eye, and the cat's body and features are highlighted with stem stitch. The sweet calico print adds character to the cat's face. I chose this fabric because it reminded me of my little white cat named Sugar. She falls asleep on my quilts, burrowing inside them when she gets cold. If I can't find her, I look for the lump!

I wanted garden angels in my quilt and decided to make them part of the label on the back of the quilt. I drew simple cookie-cutter-style shapes for the head, body, and wings. Margaret suggested adding French knots for the hair as a surprise element. I did the lettering by hand, using a computer printout as a template.

Lynn Todoroff did the machine quilting for me. She is a whiz, and I love her ideas for quilting. First, she outline-stitched all of the appliqué shapes. The plaid grid stitched on point in the background mimics the diagonal lines in the corner post fabric. Leaves and vines tie the various design areas together, extending the garden theme without detracting from the hearts and their appliqués. The name of the quilt runs across the top in raspberry red stitching.

Garden Sweet Garden

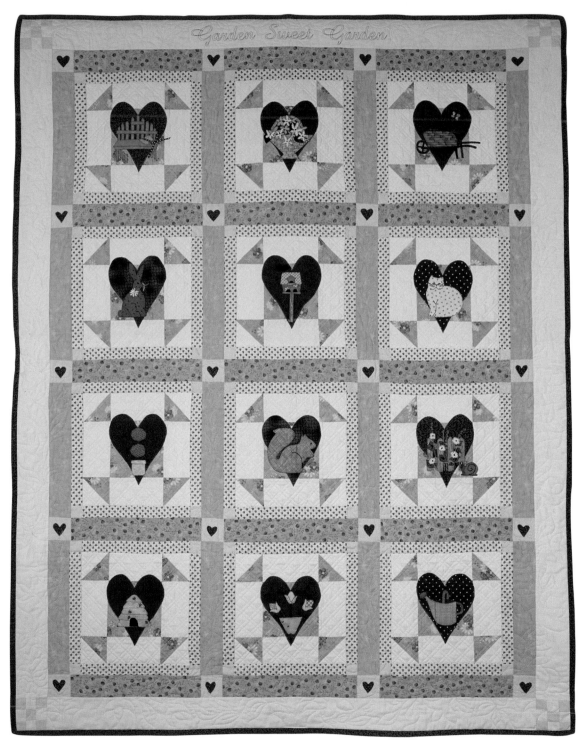

Pieced and appliquéd by Anne Sutton; machine-quilted by Lynn Todoroff; 50½" x 64½".

♥ MATERIALS

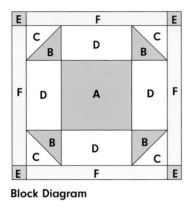

Block Diagram

⅝ yard for A and B

1½ yards for C, D, Nine-Patches, and outer border

⅜ yard for E, corner posts, and Nine-Patches

⅝ yard for F

½ yard for vertical sashing

½ yard for horizontal sashing

½ yard total of six different red prints for the hearts

½ yard red for binding

Assorted scraps in warm brown, white, dark green, soft gold, and black for appliqués

3¼ yards backing

¼ yard narrow ribbon to trim hat

3 yards paper-backed fusible web

10" square for label background, plus scraps for appliqués

55" x 69" batting

Embroidery floss in green, black, white, and yellow

Two appliqué nonstick pressing sheets

♥ CUTTING

Refer to the block diagram above.

For A, cut two 5½" x 42" strips; cut into twelve 5½" squares.

For B and C, cut two 3⅜" x 42" strips from each fabric. Place each B strip on a C strip, right sides together. Cut into twenty-four 3⅜" squares; then cut diagonally into half-square triangles (48 layered triangles total). Do not separate the layers.

For D, cut seven 3" x 42" strips; cut into forty-eight 3" x 5½" pieces.

For E, cut two 1½" x 42" strips; cut into forty-eight 1½" squares.

For F, cut twelve 1½" x 42" strips; cut into forty-eight 1½" x 10½" pieces.

For the vertical quilt sashing, cut six 2½" x 42" strips; cut into sixteen 2½" x 12½" pieces.

For the horizontal quilt sashing, cut five 2½" x 42" strips; cut into fifteen 2½" x 12½" lengths.

For the sashing corner posts, cut two 2½" strips; cut into twenty 2½" squares.

For the outer borders, cut six 3½" x 42" strips. Piece together end to end and cut two 3½" x 58½" strips for the side outer borders and two 3½" x 44½" strips for the top and bottom outer borders.

For the Nine-Patch border corners, cut twenty 1½" squares from the corner post fabric and sixteen 1½" squares from the border fabric.

Photocopy the appliqué patterns (pages 40–43). Trace 12 large hearts and 20 small hearts onto paper-backed fusible web. Fuse to the red fabrics. Cut out all the hearts. The remaining appliqués will be prepared in step 4.

♥ INSTRUCTIONS

1. Stitch the half-square triangles together as paired to make 4 BC units per block, or 48 total. Press toward the darker fabric. Stitch a BC unit to each end of a D piece. Stitch a D piece to either side of an A piece. Join the BCD and AD units as shown to construct 12 blocks. Press.

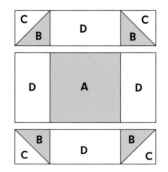

2. Stitch an E square to each end of 24 F strips. Press. Add 2 F strips and 2 EF units to each of the blocks as shown. Press.

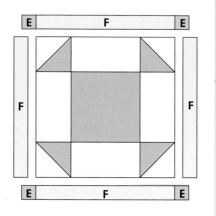

3. Fuse a large heart to the middle of each block, following the manufacturer's instructions. Fuse a small heart to the middle of each 2$\frac{1}{2}$-inch-square sashing corner post.

4. To prepare the remaining appliqués, trace each shape individually onto paper-backed fusible web, observing the overlap lines on the patterns. Try to group together shapes that will be fused to the same fabric. Fuse to the appropriate fabrics, cut out on the marked lines, and remove the paper backing. Also prepare 1 heart and 3 angel appliqués for the label, if desired; set these aside.

5. Fuse single-fabric appliqués, such as the squirrel, directly to a block, as you did the hearts. For more complex appliqués, place the appliqué pattern on a light table, lay an appliqué pressing sheet on top, and arrange the cutout pieces on it.

Cover with a second pressing sheet and press lightly. Let cool. Now you can peel the entire appliqué off the pressing sheet and fuse it to the block as a unit. Use this method to keep small appliqué pieces positioned properly.

6. Work buttonhole stitch around the edges of each appliqué by hand or by machine. I used a machine blanket stitch. Follow the instructions in your sewing machine manual to see how you might achieve a similar effect.

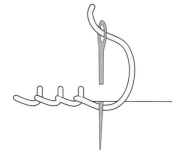

Buttonhole Stitch

7. Add details to the appliqués using hand embroidery. Use stem stitch for flower stems, stalks, and other lines you wish to accentuate. Work French knots for animal eyes, flower centers, buds, and the dots at the ends of the snail's antennae. Embroider lazy daisy stitch petals and satin-stitch leaves for the bunny's flower.

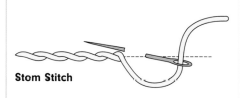

Stom Stitch

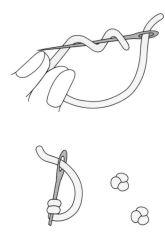

French Knot

Lazy Daisy Stitch

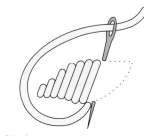

Satin Stitch

8. Join the quilt blocks, sashing, and corner posts as shown. Press.

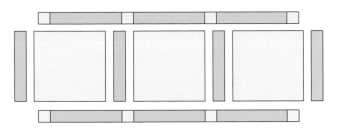

9. Using the 1$\frac{1}{2}$" squares, make four Nine-Patch blocks for the border corners as shown. Press.

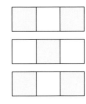

10. Add the side borders to the quilt. Press. Stitch a Nine-Patch block to each end of the top and bottom border strips. Press. Add the top and bottom borders to the quilt. Press.

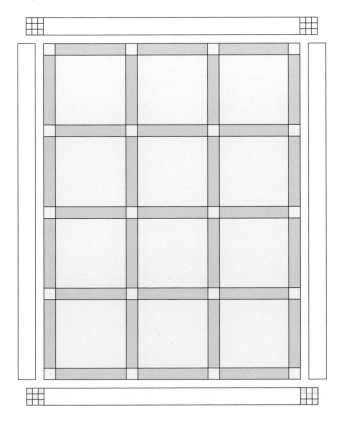

11. Layer and finish the quilt. Lynn Todoroff machine-quilted a plaid grid in the main section of each block and vines in the sashing and borders. The words "Garden Sweet Garden" are machine-stitched across the top border. See the journal for more details.

Vine Quilting Design
Enlarge to desired size

Plaid Quilting Design

12. To make a label, type your information on a computer and make an actual-size printout. Place the printout on a light table, lay the label appliqués from step 4 on top, and trace the lettering with a black fine-tip permanent marker. Follow the step 5 technique to appliqué the heart and angels to the label background fabric (a 10" square). Embroider French knots for hair. Fold in the edges of the label all around and blind-stitch to the back of the quilt.

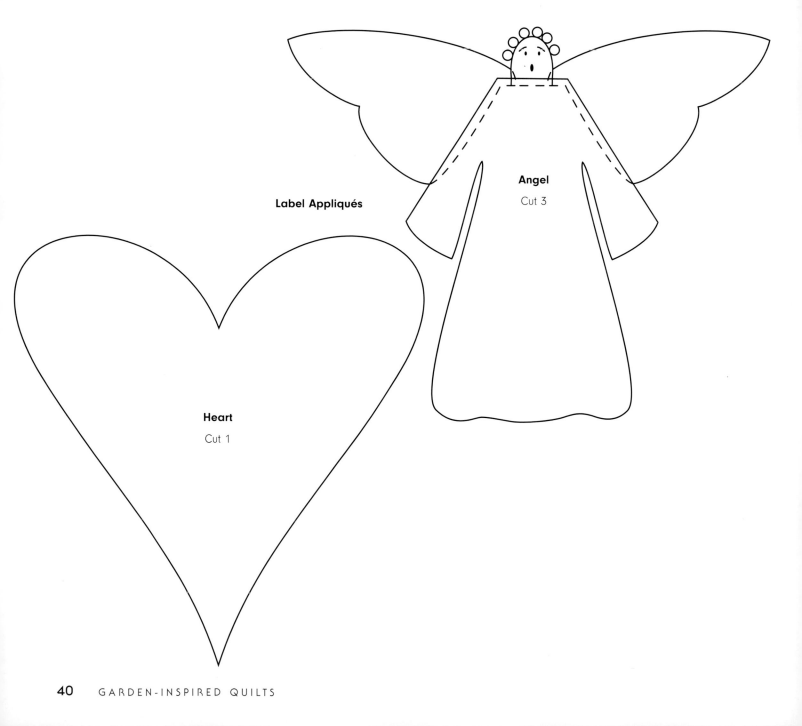

Label Appliqués

Angel
Cut 3

Heart
Cut 1

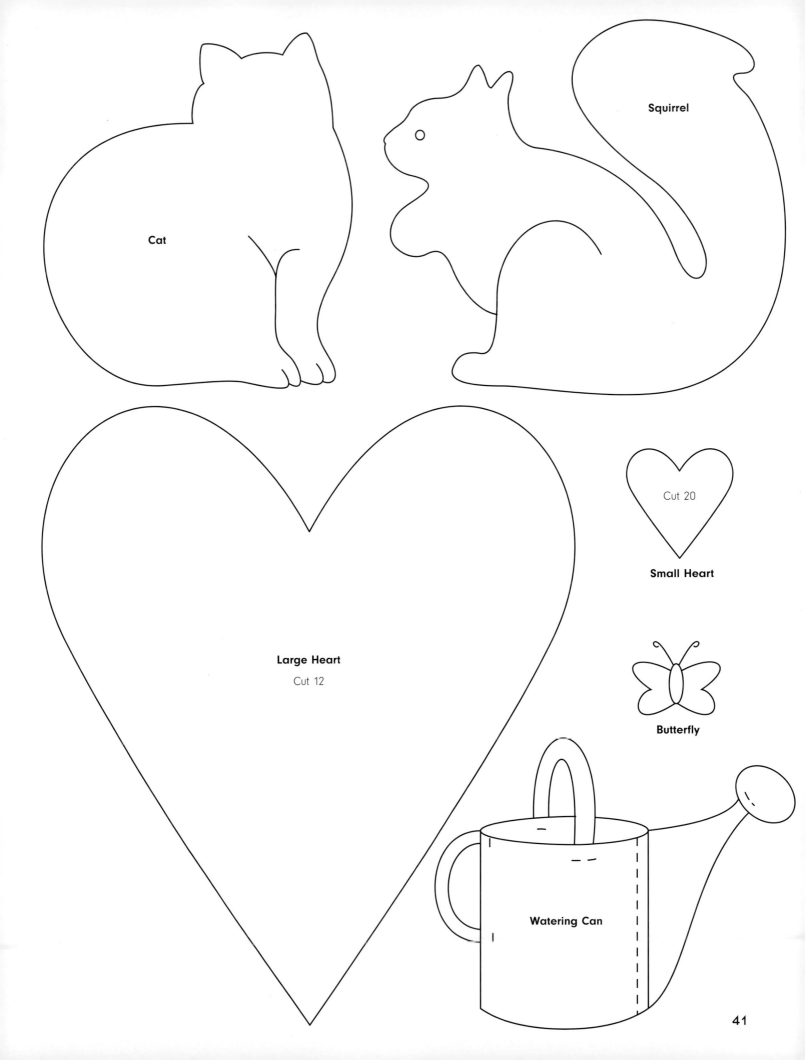

Cat

Squirrel

Cut 20

Small Heart

Butterfly

Large Heart

Cut 12

Watering Can

41

Hat

Flower Basket

Beehive

Wheelbarrow

Leaves

Bench

Flowerpot

Rabbit

Bird

Snail

Birdhouse

Fence

Topiary

Garden Friends

BY ANNE SUTTON

My husband and I are animal lovers, and *Garden Friends* was designed with animals in mind. Our house is currently home to ten cats. (Nine at the time I designed the quilt, so nine hearts on the tree.) All but one are "rescue" kitties. Our kitties are so spoiled, they don't remember being homeless. Their favorite pastime is lounging at the windows, watching the squirrels outside in the garden.

My sewing machine sits on a corner table by the window, overlooking the garden. We have a very large tree with two attached squirrel feeders, and as I sew, I am simultaneously entertained by squirrel antics. We buy peanuts by the case and store them outside in a large garbage can. The squirrels know where we keep the peanuts and try to outsmart us. Our first can was plastic, and they chewed right through the lid. Now we have a metal can and a bungee cord to secure the lid. Several of the squirrels have become very tame and let me walk right up to them.

In my quilt, I decided to show the view from my sewing room into the garden. A red-checked square became the "window" looking out to the tree and the squirrels that play there. Mr. Max, the cat I placed under the tree, has given up trying to catch them. (Our newest arrival, Mr. Lucky, is not as smart. He spends most of his day "squirreling.")

I especially love the crisp, country look of red-and-white check, and I paired up a darker red and white for the two outer borders to accentuate the contrast. My husband and son could not believe I was using red and white in a squirrel quilt. They pictured the squirrels with furlike fabrics and lots of brown acorns. Well, I won, and my squirrels are done in cute country prints, though I compromised a little with some beige.

To find a combination of prints for the squirrels and the acorns, I hunted through my fabric stash. Once I had a working palette, I started pairing up prints for the acorns. For several, I chose stripes to create a linear effect. For the squirrels, I looked to warm brown prints and plaids. Each squirrel combines two different fabrics, and the tail detailing and hearts gave me an opportunity to use red again. For the tree, I was fortunate to find a warm brown with subtle black wood-grain lines. A yellow calico seemed fitting for Mr. Max.

To accentuate the folk art look of the quilt, I chose to buttonhole-stitch the appliqués using a heavy Madeira Cotona machine thread. Black thread, my usual choice, would have been too dark against the beige fabrics; for a softer look, I used a warm brown thread color instead. I fused the appliqués to the individual blocks, worked the buttonhole stitch, and then joined the blocks together.

Lynn Todoroff machine-quilted the upside-down heart motifs throughout the center block. As this shape is echoed, it subtly repeats and calls attention to the heart appliqués in the tree. The surrounding blocks are tightly stippled in a random pattern. I love the continuously stitched red hearts in the border and the way they echo the heart theme.

Labels are an essential part of the quiltmaking process for me. I think about the label design while I am working on the quilt. I type the wording on the computer and make a printout. Then I lay the printout on my light table, put fabric over the top, and trace the wording with a permanent black marker. Adding the label last, by hand, after the layers are quilted and bound, always gives me a sense of completion.

Garden Friends

Pieced and appliquéd by Anne Sutton; machine-quilted by Lynn Todoroff; 48½" x 48½".

MATERIALS

2 yards for background

$^3/_8$ yard for inner border

$^5/_8$ yard for second border and binding

$^1/_2$ yard wood-grain fabric for tree

$^1/_4$ yard for hearts

$^1/_8$ yard for leaves

$^1/_4$ yard for cat

1 yard total of assorted tan, brown, and red scraps for appliqués

Yellow scrap for star

3 yards paper-backed fusible web

3 yards backing

9" square for label background

53" x 53" batting

Madeira Cotona thread or brown embroidery floss

CUTTING

Photocopy patterns A through N (pages 51–53), enlarging as indicated. Trace A, D, F, G, and H onto paper-backed fusible web. Trace the remaining patterns onto template plastic and cut out. Use the plastic templates to mark the following on paper-backed fusible web: 28 B, 17 C, 2 E, 8 I (reverse 4), 8 J (reverse 4), 8 K, 8 L, 3 M, and 5 N. Fuse all of the pieces to the wrong side of the appropriate fabrics, and cut out. Prepare an additional large squirrel I and large squirrel tail J for the quilt label, if desired.

From the background fabric, cut one 20$^1/_2$" square for the center block, sixteen 8$^1/_2$" squares for the smaller appliqué blocks, and five 3$^1/_2$" x 42" strips. Piece the strips end to end, and cut two 3$^1/_2$" x 42$^1/_2$" strips for the top and bottom outer borders and two 3$^1/_2$" x 48$^1/_2$" strips for the side outer borders.

From inner border fabric, cut four 2$^1/_2$" x 42" strips. Cut into two 2$^1/_2$" x 20$^1/_2$" strips for the top and bottom borders and two 2$^1/_2$" x 24$^1/_2$" strips for the side borders.

From the second border fabric, cut five 1$^1/_2$" x 42" strips. Cut into two 1$^1/_2$" x 40$^1/_2$" strips for the top and bottom

borders. Piece the remaining strips end to end, and cut two 1$^1/_2$" x 42$^1/_2$" strips for the side borders.

INSTRUCTIONS

1. Lay the center block right side up. Arrange appliqué pieces A through H on the block, using the quilt photo (page 48) as a guide. Fuse in place, following the manufacturer's instructions.

2. Lay the 8$^1/_2$" squares right side up. Arrange and fuse the remaining appliqué pieces to make 8 squirrel blocks and 8 acorn blocks.

3. Work a machine buttonhole stitch around each appliqué using heavy Madeira Cotona thread. Consult your sewing machine manual for instructions. To work a buttonhole stitch by hand, use two strands of brown embroidery floss.

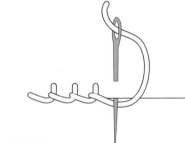

Buttonhole Stitch

4. Add the top and bottom inner borders to the center block. Press. Add the side inner borders. Press.

5. Arrange the squirrel and acorn blocks around the center block, squirrels facing toward the center. Stitch three blocks together for the top and bottom, and add to the quilt. Stitch five blocks together for each side, and add to the quilt.

6. Add the second border, the top and bottom first and then the sides. Press as you go.

7. Add the outside border, the top and bottom first and then the sides. Press as you go.

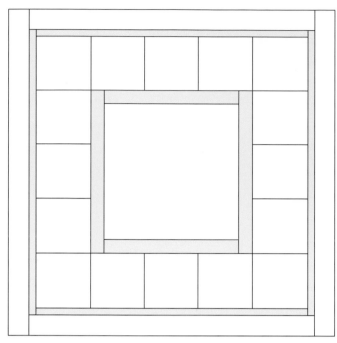

Quilt Diagram

8. Layer and finish the quilt. Lynn Todoroff machine-quilted upside-down heart motifs throughout the center block. The surrounding blocks are tightly stippled in a random pattern.

9. To make a label, type your information on a computer and make an actual-size printout. Place the printout on a light table, lay the squirrel appliqué on top, and trace the lettering with a black fine-tip permanent marker. Appliqué the squirrel and tail to the label background fabric (a 9" square). Fold in the edges of the label all around and blind-stitch to the back of the quilt.

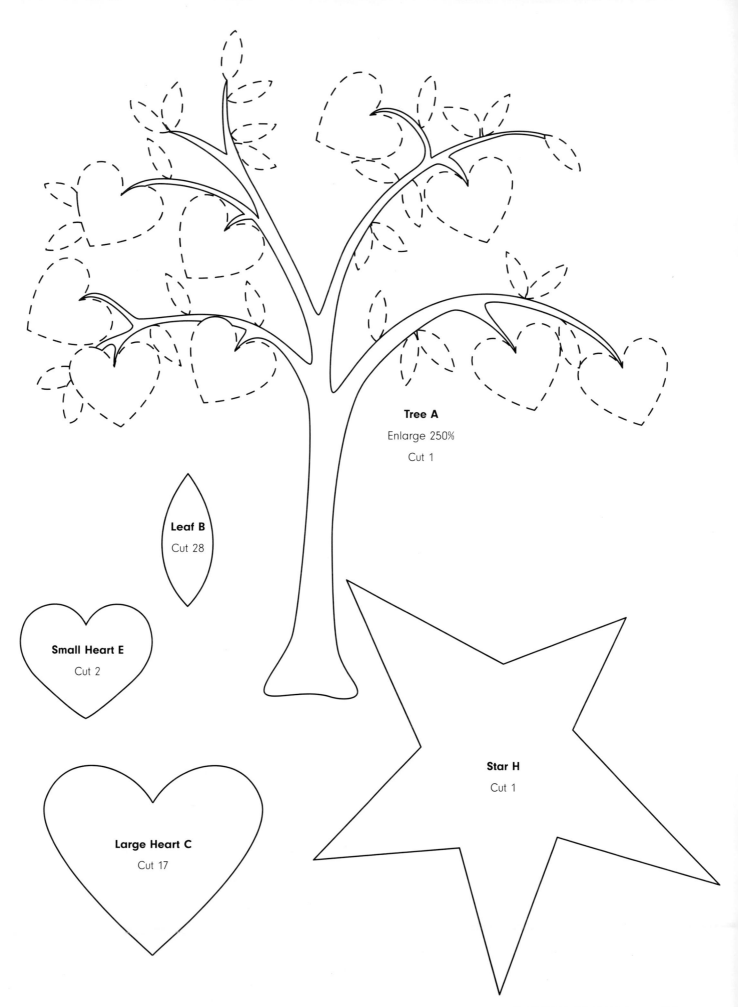

Tree A

Enlarge 250%

Cut 1

Leaf B

Cut 28

Small Heart E

Cut 2

Large Heart C

Cut 17

Star H

Cut 1

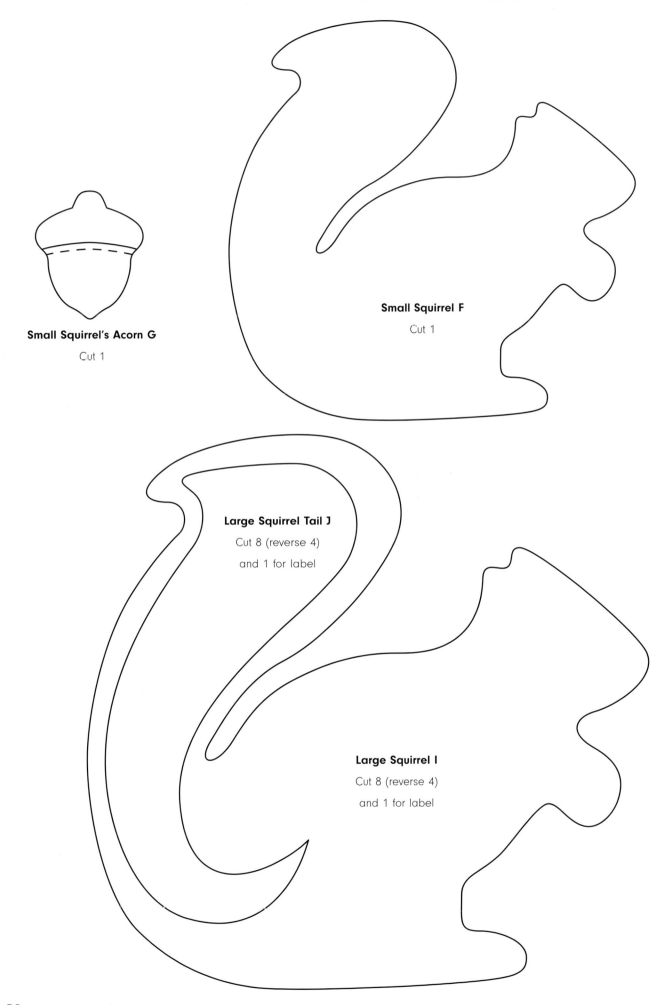

Small Squirrel's Acorn G

Cut 1

Small Squirrel F

Cut 1

Large Squirrel Tail J

Cut 8 (reverse 4)

and 1 for label

Large Squirrel I

Cut 8 (reverse 4)

and 1 for label

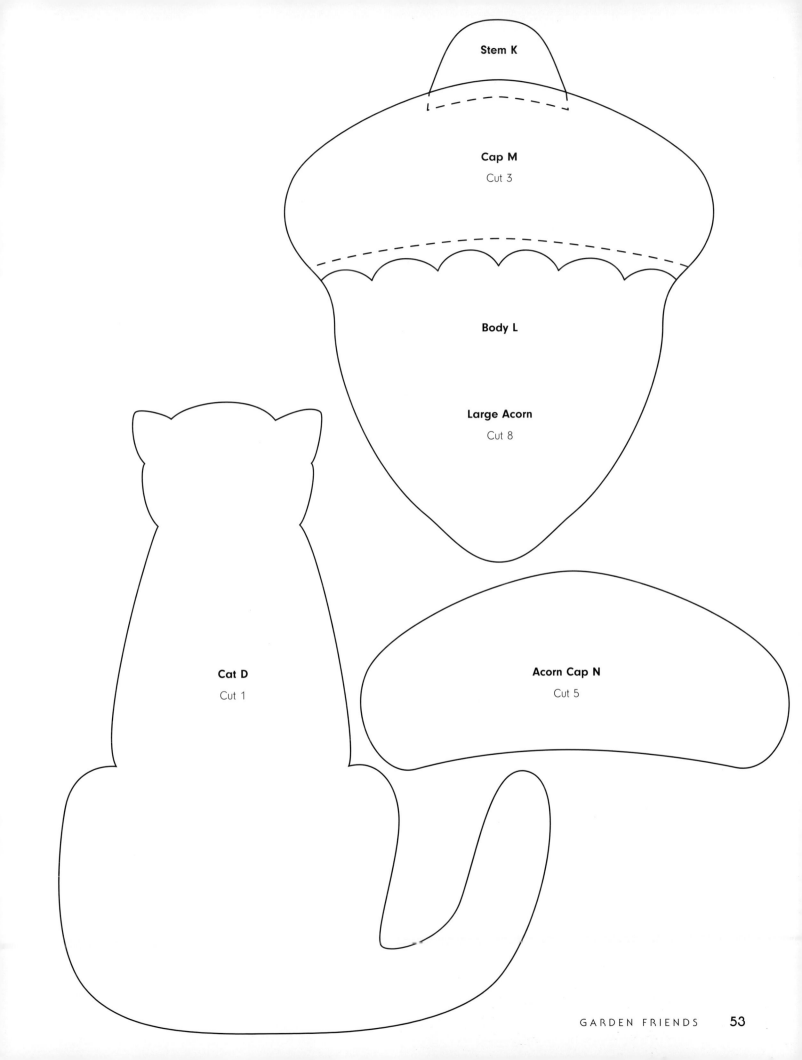

Stem K

Cap M
Cut 3

Body L

Large Acorn
Cut 8

Cat D
Cut 1

Acorn Cap N
Cut 5

Meadow Medallion

BY JEAN WELLS

Early last summer I purchased a rusted antique grille to use as a stepping stone in the garden. I was laying out the vegetable garden in a Nine-Patch grid when the idea struck me to do another quilt block planting with the medallion at the center. I prepared the soil, positioned the metal medallion, and then scattered wildflower seeds in the openings and around the edges. Before I knew it, the seeds had germinated and filled out the patch with foliage and flowers. In midsummer, I added my favorite border flower, small marigolds. The intense colors make a strong edging.

I find myself crossing back and forth between quilting and gardening almost effortlessly it seems, incorporating my quilting ideas into the garden and vice versa. The grids and block designs that I use in quilting translate perfectly to the raised beds in my vegetable garden. Last year, I took my six-inch by twenty-four-inch quilter's ruler out to the garden to lay out a grid for planting lettuce and spinach. Then I found myself arranging zinnia plants in a colorful Nine-Patch. It's fun!

All winter long, I thought about my rusty medallion nestled among the wildflowers. I wanted to interpret the entire plot in a quilt. My first impulse was to find a meadowlike printed floral for the background and to hand-appliqué the medallion shape against it in a solid color, similar to the technique used in Hawaiian quilting. Try as I might, I had no luck finding an appropriate background fabric, even though I'm the owner of a fabric store. When I explained my dilemma to Valori, she suggested piecing the background to create the right mood.

The watercolor approach to piecing, where all the squares are cut to the same size and set on point, appealed to me. The idea is to choose fabrics that "transition" from one to another, minimizing or even camouflaging the seams. I knew from past experience that the fabric choices are very important in watercolor-style quilts. In order to flow together, the fabrics need to share a common mood or appearance.

In the case of my informal wildflowers, I wanted to convey a mass of wispy stems, foliage, and flowers as well as the occasional single bloom seen up close.

Valori and I spent a few hours in the floral department of The Stitchin' Post auditioning fabrics for my quilt. Valori has a great eye, and her open mind is quick to see the possibilities. First, there was a large sunflower print that would yield bits and pieces of its flowers when cut up—in my pieced meadow, these fragments come across as larger flowers. We also found some smaller prints that would offer unique pockets of color when cut into squares. Transition fabrics, like the meadow print, have more than one color and help the eye travel "seamlessly" from block to block by creating color links. When the meadow print is cut with mostly yellow flowers showing, I can place it next to the larger-scale sunflower print and create a yellow area in the quilt. If a little pink shows in the corner, I butt that section against a pink edge in some other square.

These seven prints will flow together seamlessly.

Green prints with different sizes and types of foliage are also a must, both to give the eye a resting place and to fill out the landscape, much the way greenery functions in nature. A print with yellow-green frogs, like those I see in my garden, gives me some fun images to tuck in among the grasses. Several frogs appear in *Meadow Medallion*, and many of my garden quilts have a frog of some kind in them. Sometimes, greens turn up where I least expect them, like the greens I found in a hot pink flower print—the flower was gaudy, but the leaf texture was perfect. In this fabric selection exercise, it doesn't matter whether I love the design overall. I'm training myself to see how the fabric will look when it is cut up.

Another element I consider is the background color in the prints. I tend to favor warm greens with a hint of yellow, rather than cooler blue-greens. This doesn't mean that every fabric in the quilt is warm, only that the overall palette appears warmer. In the warm version of the quilt, fifteen to twenty percent of the fabrics are actually cool blues; in the cool quilt, there are warm yellows. Adding a smaller amount of the opposite temperature gives the quilt a sparkle. My decorator friend Janet Storton points out that the same thing is true in interiors. An all-blue room appears boring without a few warm accents.

I hit my second snag when I began tracing the medallion stepping stone to make a pattern. It was not symmetrical. To even things up, I isolated a one-eighth wedge to use as a pattern. I cut a large paper circle the same size as the medallion and folded it into eighths. Then I opened the paper up and retraced the wedge pattern in all eight sections, connecting the lines across the folds.

My next decision was to determine the quilt size over-all—too large, and the medallion would appear unim-portant; too small, and it would be overpowering. Once again, I turned to a photograph of the real garden for visual reference. I rely on my natural eye when it comes to judging proportions.

Another size decision concerned the fabric squares that are repeated across the quilt. They needed to be small enough to give lots of places for different fabrics but not so small that there would be too many seams. After experimenting and looking at other watercolor-style quilts, I decided on a two-inch finished square, or two and seven-eighths inches high when set on point. Splitting the squares diagonally would increase the detail, but I didn't think I'd go this route since I would be putting the medallion on top of the pieced meadow.

Once the parameters of the quilt were set, I was off and running. I pinned my reference photographs to the wall for inspiration and laid out the fabric pieces on a flannel board. I used the mostly green prints around the edges as a natural frame for the quilt. Then I worked in more greens, adding squares with a bit of color. If there was yellow in the green print, I could move to a larger-scale print with more yellow for a neighboring square. In this way, I was able to create pockets of color across the surface. My one remaining challenge was to place some tiny blue wildflowers in the quilt. I was unable to find a blue print with the right green in the background. I settled on a yellow background print with some blue flowers and a blue background print with some yellow and red flowers. As it turns out, these fab-rics lighten up the center of the quilt.

Appliquéing the medallion came last. The deep dark green fabric I had originally planned to use wasn't right against the pieced background. The green had too much blue and black in it. Referring to the photographs, I recalled that what I had liked about the metal stepping stone in the first place was its rusty color. Out came a piece of hand-painted fabric I had purchased from Just Imagination. The hue was right, and subtle changes in the dye made it look rusty.

Perhaps it was the difficulty I had choosing a color for the medallion, but the idea popped into my head to try the same design in a cool palette. In the blue version of the quilt, with yellows and lighter blues predominant in the background, the dark green medallion worked exceptionally well. Making two color versions, one warm and the other cool, helped me understand how temperature works in quilts and how it influences the overall mood.

Meadow Medallion

Designed and made by Jean Wells; 30½" x 30½".

▓ MATERIALS

¹/₈ yard each of twelve to fourteen different fabrics for the background watercolor squares (I used greens, pinks, yellows, some blue, and a little white, inspired by my meadow photograph.)

⁵/₈ yard for setting triangles and corners

³/₄ yard for the medallion and binding

1 yard paper-backed fusible web

1 yard backing

35" x 35" batting

Flannel design wall

▓ CUTTING

For the watercolor squares, cut one 2¹/₂" strip from each fabric to start. Cut into 2¹/₂" squares and stack like fabrics together. Cut more squares as needed.

For the setting triangles, cut nine 7" squares. Cut into quarter-square triangles.

For the corners, cut two 4" squares; then cut diagonally.

For the medallion, make eight photocopies of the wedge pattern (page 61). Cut out the wedges and tape them together to make a medallion pattern. Trace the medallion onto paper-backed fusible web. Fuse to the medallion fabric and cut out, using small, sharp scissors for the interior shapes.

Completed Medallion Pattern

▓ INSTRUCTIONS

1. Establish the diagonal grid by placing any ten 2¹/₂" squares on point across the top of the design wall. In the same way, place ten squares on point down one side. Fill out the design area with additional squares, as if you were putting together a puzzle. Rearrange the squares until you are satisfied with the color flow and placement. I placed the greens around the edges and worked the yellows and blues toward the center. If you need inspiration, reread the journal discussion about the watercolor quilt technique.

Lay out the squares on point across the top and down one side.

Place more squares on point to fill in the diagonal grid.

2. Once the squares are in place, insert the setting triangles. Note that they will overlap. Add the four corners.

3. To join the squares, begin at any corner. Piece the first diagonal row, including the setting triangles at each end. Press all the seams in one direction. Piece the second diagonal row, including the setting triangles. Press all the seams in the opposite direction.

Sew the first two rows together, butting the seams and overlapping the triangle points. Trim the overlapped points. Continue in this way until the entire quilt is pieced. Add the corner triangles. Press. Apply spray starch to the quilt top; I find it stabilizes the fabrics and makes for easier machine quilting.

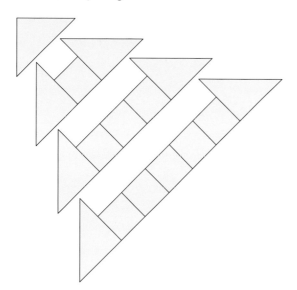

Piece each diagonal row, including the setting triangles at each end.

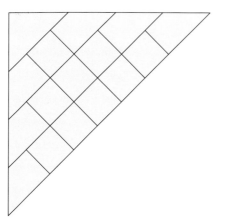

Join the diagonal rows, overlapping the triangle points.

4. Fold the pieced quilt top in half each way to find the center. Mark the center and the middle of each edge with a pin. Lay the quilt top right side up on a flat pressing surface. Center the medallion right side up on top, aligning it with the pin markers. Fuse in place, following the manufacturer's instructions. Blind-stitch or satin-stitch the outer edges, if desired.

The pieced quilt top.

5. Trim the quilt top evenly around the edges. Layer and finish the quilt. Outline-stitch around the edge of the medallion. Quilt small leaves around the medallion.

The cool palette version of *Meadow Medallion*.

Quilting Design

Enlarge to desired size

Medallion Wedge Pattern

Make 8 copies and tape them together

Angels

BY JEAN WELLS

Folk art angels occupy several places in my garden—my favorite is among the sunflowers. Because I see my angels day after day, I guess I'm not surprised that their shapes have stuck with me, ready to resurface from my subconscious. This past winter when Valori's brand-new "Harmonies" batik fabrics arrived at the store, I was itching to start a new quilt. Angels seemed like the perfect theme.

I got the new fabric home and immediately laid it out to study. I saw at once that if I cut this beautiful fabric into small pieces, the large sunflower and leaf designs would be lost. My desire was to preserve them, as they would be perfect for free-motion quilting later on. I had another motive for showing Valori's "Harmonies" fabrics to advantage. If I used them, this quilt could become my challenge quilt for our annual Stitchin' Post exhibit at the Sisters Outdoor Quilt Show.

My first step was to see if an angel shape would lend itself to the batik fabric designs. To make a pattern, I folded a large sheet of paper in half lengthwise and sketched half of an angel. Then I cut through both layers and unfolded the paper to see what I had come up with. I made the angel dress and wings deliberately simple. I don't have much skill or confidence in the drawing department, and it took a few tries before I felt I had gotten the proportions right. I convinced myself that if I kept the shapes basic, the fabrics would do the work. For a halo, I let the sunflower petals inspire me, but I simplified them, too.

Picking out fabrics was fun! I began by choosing four background fabrics, two light and two dark. As I auditioned fabrics for the angels, I felt like I was back making paper dolls or sewing doll clothes. I let the fabrics speak to me in terms of design as well as color. I tried to be brave with color and to put unusual things together. At the same time, I was considering how various sections of the print would fit my angel shapes and how they would look when outline-quilted. My confidence in making these types of decisions is much greater than it was a couple of years ago. I think of myself as a detective, observing nature and found objects for clues, taking note of every nuance. I'm still very interested in individual colors and patterns, but I've also become a keen observer of how they relate to one another.

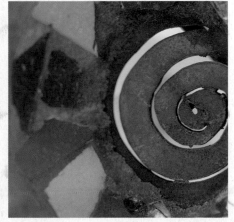

Several metal sunflower sculptures by Mary Taylor of the Rosebar Company are "planted" in my garden. Last year, I decided to put the metal sunflowers in with the live sunflowers. The effect was stunning, not to mention continually evolving. In the beginning, the metal sculptures towered over the young plants. As the sunflowers grew taller, the shapes played off one another, and the metal flowers were eventually engulfed by the crowd. By summer's end, when the real flowers had gone to seed and the stems were withering, the metal structures proudly stood their ground.

Images like these come to mind in the winter when there is snow on the ground and I am in my quilting studio dreaming of summer gardening. I enjoy gardening so much, these mental images are very strong and intense. I rely on them to tell me about mood and feeling. For technical information about shapes and colors, I turn to my snapshots and Valori's photographs.

A snapshot helped me re-create the sunflowers from my summer garden for my quilt. To make a pattern, I traced a sunflower from the photograph and enlarged it on a photocopier. As usual, it was necessary to simplify the line drawing to make it suitable for appliqué.

Sunflower centers intrigue me, and I wondered how I might capture their richness. As I studied my reference photos, I came away thinking that simple wedges in a variety of brown shades would convey the complex texture. To play out this idea, I used Valori's "stitch 'n flip" technique—a way of foundation-piecing on a precut muslin shape.

The angels' folk art sensibility called out for a simple setting. At this point, I got out graph paper and started evaluating the proportions. The dimensions of the four rectangular background blocks were determined by the size and shape of the angel. The blocks needed breathing room, but I didn't want them floating. A wider sashing in the center would give my appliquéd sunflower a place to set down roots.

I next added a simple border but found it boring. Back to my reference photographs. I came across a wonderful picture of wildflowers. What struck me was the little pockets of bright, intense color among all these different greens. Valori's batik line had some bright pinks, oranges, blues, and purples. Scattering them at random in a double row of squares let me create a meadowlike border. Greens predominate, and the bright colors appear as little jewels in the landscape. This multicolored border pulls in and repeats all of the colors in the quilt, plus a few others.

I could hardly wait to start quilting. The designs in the batiks got me started with the free-motion quilting, just as I had suspected they would. From there, I carried out those same shapes in the background areas of the blocks. This type of subtle repetition leads to unity in the overall design. I stitched simple leaves and vines in the backgrounds and borders. I found myself inventing swirls to fill in solid areas. Then I took the swirl idea and expanded on it, making everything larger.

Angels

Designed and made by Jean Wells; 54½" x 64½".

✳ MATERIALS

²⁄₃ yard each of four different background fabrics (two light and two dark)

⁵⁄₈ yard for sashing and border squares

¹⁄₃ yard each of eight different fabrics for the angel wings, dresses, and border squares

³⁄₈ yard each of three different yellow fabrics for halos and sunflowers

1 yard assorted green fabrics for stems, leaves, and binding

Scraps of brown fabrics for sunflower centers

¹⁄₄ yard muslin for foundation piecing

¹⁄₈ yard for angel faces

³⁄₄ yard assorted fabrics for pieced border (and use leftover angel and sashing fabrics)

3¹⁄₃ yards backing

59" x 69" batting

✳ CUTTING

For the angel backgrounds, cut four 21¹⁄₂" x 27¹⁄₂" pieces.

Cut two 2¹⁄₂" x 21¹⁄₂" strips for the horizontal sashing. Cut two 4¹⁄₂" x 42" strips, piece together end to end, and cut one 4¹⁄₂" x 56¹⁄₂" vertical sashing strip.

Enlarge patterns A through I (pages 71–73) 200%. Cut out each pattern piece individually on the marked lines (use two photocopies for the sunflower petals). To use the patterns, pin them to the appropriate fabric at least ¹⁄₂" apart. Cut out each piece ¹⁄₄" beyond the pattern edges all around.

Cut out pieces A through E for four angels from various fabrics.

Cut out enough petals for two F sunflowers and three G sunflowers. Cut two F and three G sunflower centers from muslin. The stems will be cut later.

Cut out five H/I pairs from different greens for the leaves.

For the border, cut the assorted fabric scraps into 2¹⁄₂" squares. You will need a total of 220 squares, but cut a few extra to give yourself some choices.

✳ INSTRUCTIONS

1. Arrange the angel appliqués A through E on the four background blocks. Hand-baste in place. To needleturn-appliqué a piece, fold under a small section of the edge, finger-pressing to give the fabric a little memory. Bring the needle up from the back of the fabric, and catch one or two threads on the underside of the fold. Insert the needle directly down through the background fabric and pull through to the wrong side, so that the stitch is concealed. Continue stitching around the appliqué shape, about ³⁄₁₆" at a time, using the point of the needle to turn under the raw edge of the appliqué as you go. Clip the inside curves as you come to them so that the appliqué lies flat. Appliqué the wings, dress outer edge, and dress center panel first. Then add the halo and face.

Needleturn Appliqué

2. Lay out the four quilt blocks, alternating the background colors as shown in the quilt photo (page 67). Join the blocks to the two horizontal sashing strips. Press. Then add the vertical sashing strip. Press.

3. For each side border, sew 28 border squares into a strip, make a second strip in a different color sequence, and then join the two strips together. Repeat to make the top and bottom borders, using 27 border squares per strip. Add the side borders to the quilt. Press. Add the top and bottom borders. Press.

Quilt Diagram

4. To begin a sunflower center, place a small triangle of brown fabric in the center of muslin piece F or G. Place a small strip of fabric in a slightly different shade of brown on the triangle, right sides together, matching one raw edge. Stitch $\frac{1}{4}$" from the raw edge through all layers. Flip the strip over and press. Trim the strip diagonally to make a triangle shape. Add a third strip, stitch, flip, and press. Trim to form a triangle.

Start with a triangle in the center.

Stitch, flip, press, and trim.

5. Continue to stitch and flip new brown strips to the block, trimming them to form triangles. Build out from the first triangle in all directions, letting the raw edges extend beyond the muslin. When the muslin is covered, press and starch the piece. Trim off the excess fabric even with the muslin edge. Repeat for each sunflower center.

6. Stitch leaf sections H and I together in pairs with a $\frac{1}{4}$" seam allowance, easing around the curve. Press the seam allowance toward the darker fabric.

7. Arrange the five sunflower centers and their petals on the quilt, allowing one flower to extend onto the top border. Pin the pieces in place. Lay the green stem fabric on the quilt top to determine the stem length, and hand-cut a strip 2" to 2$\frac{1}{2}$" wide (the width after appliquéing will be about $\frac{1}{2}$" less). Add the five leaves. Hand-baste and needleturn-appliqué all the pieces.

8. Layer and finish the quilt. Use the quilting designs on the next page.

Quilting Designs

Enlarge to desired size

Wing

Leaf Detail

Leaf for Background

Star

Dress Detail

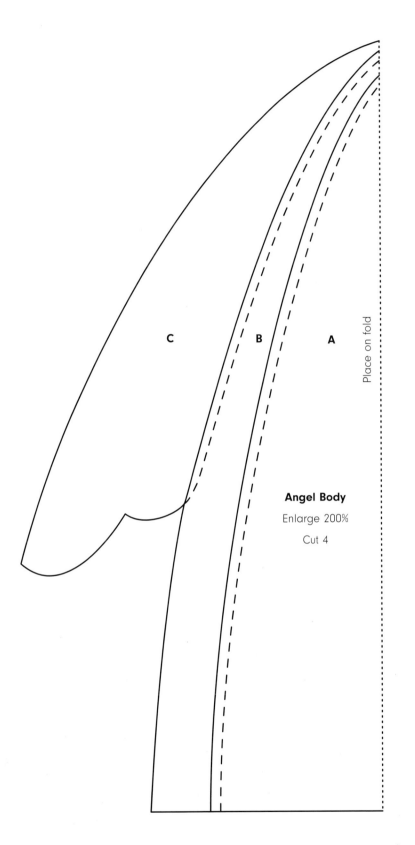

Angel Body

Enlarge 200%

Cut 4

C

B

A

Place on fold

Note: To use these patterns for the *Vintage Angel* quilt, see cutting instructions on page 75.

Large Sunflower F

Enlarge 200%

Cut 2

Angel Face E

Enlarge 200%

Cut 4

Note: To use these patterns for the *Vintage Angel* quilt, see cutting instructions on page 75.

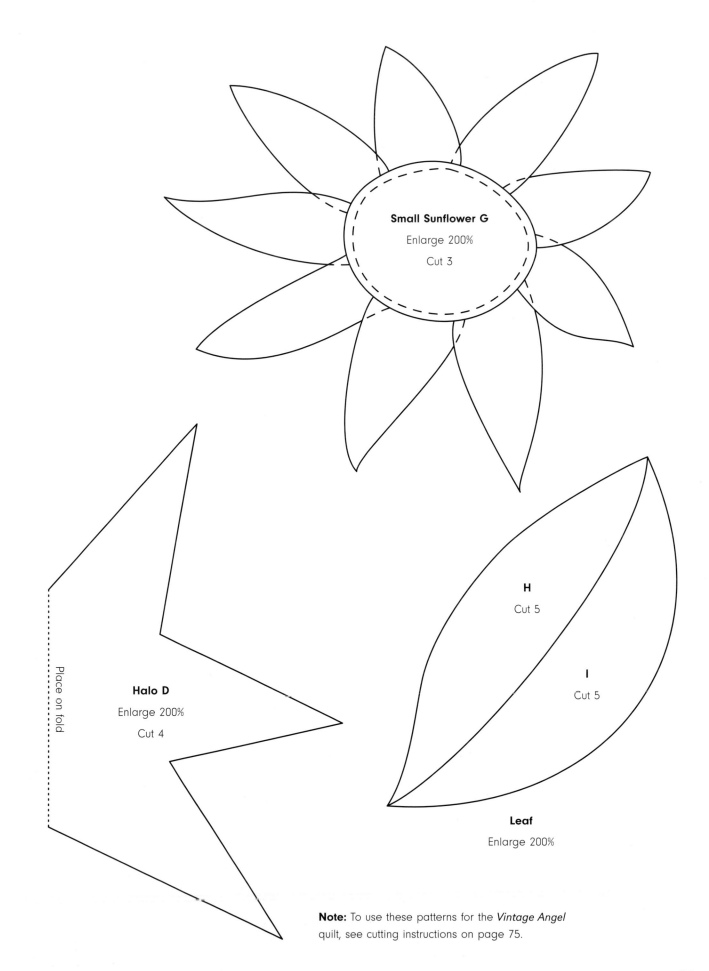

Small Sunflower G

Enlarge 200%

Cut 3

H
Cut 5

I
Cut 5

Place on fold

Halo D

Enlarge 200%

Cut 4

Leaf

Enlarge 200%

Note: To use these patterns for the *Vintage Angel* quilt, see cutting instructions on page 75.

Vintage Angel

BY BARBARA FERGUSON

Vintage textiles are my favorite fabrics to work with in quilting, and when I saw the angel quilt Jean had designed, my thoughts immediately flew to that style of fabric. For my quilt, I placed a single angel alongside a towering sunflower. Since most sunflowers are tall and the flower heads droop as they become heavy with seeds, I made mine this way. The beautiful varieties of sunflowers grown today inspired the rust and gold palette.

Choosing clothes for the angel gave me the most fun. I fussy-cut a large floral print for the center panel to feature precisely the area of the flower arrangement that I liked. Two outer panels echo the palette with a different print. The wings needed to be a stronger color to stand out. Everything shows up against the light background—a homespun fabric with small wheat-colored flecks showing up in the weave.

Buttonhole stitch is my choice for appliqué, especially in folk art quilts. Instead of matching the embroidery thread to the fabric, I chose black. Gerri Moore did the stitching for me.

I had liked what Jean did with the double row of squares for her quilt border, but two rows on my quilt was too much. I settled on a single row of one-inch squares, cutting them—as did Jean—from the leftover appliqué fabrics. The binding gave me another chance to use the green stem and leaf fabric.

To quilt this piece, I first outlined the appliquéd shapes. Then I echoed the stitching in the flowers and stem. In the background, I let the subtle pattern in the fabric suggest stitching lines.

Vintage Angel

Made by Barbara Ferguson; embroidered by Gerri Moore; 23½" x 27½".

![] MATERIALS

²/₃ yard for background
The following yardage amounts include enough fabric for the appliqué shapes and the squares in the border. The shapes are small, so fabric scraps could easily be substituted.
¼ yard for dress center panel
¼ yard for dress side panels
¼ yard for wings
⅓ yard for halo
⅛ yard for face
½ yard for sunflower stem, leaves, and binding
⅛ yard of two different fabrics for the sunflower petals

⅛ yard each of two different fabrics for the sunflower centers
¾ yard backing
2 yards paper-backed fusible web
28" x 32" batting
Black embroidery floss

![] CUTTING

For the background, cut a 21½" x 25½" piece.
Enlarge patterns A through I (pages 71–73) 150%. Trace patterns A through G once onto paper-backed fusible web, completing the half-patterns as indicated; trace six leaf outlines.

Cut out the individual pieces and fuse to the appropriate fabric following the manufacturer's instructions.
For the border, cut ninety-six 1½" squares from the appliqué fabric scraps, plus a few extras for more color choices.

![] INSTRUCTIONS

1. Referring to the quilt photo, arrange the angel, leaf, and sunflower appliqués on the background, overlapping as necessary. Draw a sunflower stem freehand on paper. Trace it onto paper-backed fusible web, being sure to reverse the image. Fuse to the green fabric and cut out. Fuse all the pieces in place following the manufacturer's instructions.

2. For each side border, sew 25 border squares together into a strip. For the top and bottom borders, sew 23 squares together into strips. Add the side borders to the quilt. Press. Add the top and bottom borders. Press.

3. Work buttonhole stitch with black floss around the edges of the appliqués.

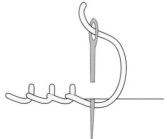

Buttonhole Stitch

4. Layer and finish the quilt.

Gerber Daisy

BY VALORI WELLS

The Gerber daisy is one of my favorite flowers. Pots and pots of them are available at the garden centers in the early spring, while we are still waiting for our daffodils to bloom. It seems that every year Mom and I buy more and more Gerbers to bring spring closer. I love to photograph this flower—the variety in the centers, petals, and colors is endless.

When the bud first emerges, it is simple and green, and then suddenly it explodes into brilliant color. Gerber colors include white, yellow, orange, pink, and red, plus many variations of those colors. Photographing the flowers gives me the chance to see the interesting shapes and colors up close and to study the graceful way the leaves unfold from the base.

As I photographed one Gerber flower after another, it occurred to me that they would make a great quilt. The struggle, of course, would be figuring out how to depict the flower. What sort of process should I try? What would interpret the Gerber the way I see it? I contemplated strip-piecing individual petals and appliquéing them down, a technique Mom used in *Zinnias*. That approach seemed adequate but not perfect for this flower.

Then I started thinking about the curved piecing techniques used by Ruth McDowell, Joen Wolfrom, and Judy Dales. Perhaps there was something here that I could make work. I was a little intimidated by curves but remembered Mom's advice about curves working if they are gentle.

I began looking at the flower again, to see where the seams might fall. Even though the Gerber wasn't perfectly symmetrical in nature, I figured I could simplify my design by drafting and repeating just a quarter of it. A quarter-pattern approach would let me cover a large area with less technical drafting. I sat down with a piece of paper the same size I wanted to make the finished flower. Rather than dividing the paper into four squares, I drew lines diagonally from corner to corner to make quarter-square triangles. I wanted the flower petals to move in a circle, and I was guessing that this division would allow for more graceful transitions.

As I fine-tuned my design, I discovered that I preferred dots to slash marks for matching up the curves. Dots seemed more accurate to me. Since I was tackling a technique that I was a little nervous about, I figured the easier I made it on myself, the better. To make the individual templates, I traced each piece individually and then added a quarter-inch seam allowance, using a flexible curve ruler on the curves. Once the templates were made, I was able to cut out and stitch the quilt in one day. Such quick progress got me thinking about working up the same design into a bed quilt.

As I was designing and piecing the flower, I was also thinking ahead to the quilting. I was already envisioning stitching to convey the growth of the petals out from the center. A combination of stitching and beads would convey the rich texture of the flower center. I think I was more excited at the prospect of quilting the flower than I was piecing it.

It was with the future quilting in mind that I chose to hand-dye my own fabric rather than use a commercial print. I wanted to convey a certain realism in the flower petals, and I didn't want a print detracting from my quilting stitches. (I also love to dye fabric, and this palette offered a new challenge.)

Once I had the flower done, I faced the question of the borders. The wood frame around one of my photographs came to mind, and I started thinking about ways to replicate it, once again using a combination of fabric and quilting stitches. With the frame added, there was still something missing. The quilt seemed blah, and I felt disappointed. Back to my photographs for clues. I felt a little stupid that I didn't see it before: Leaves! The quilt needed leaves, not just for color but also for their shape. With leaves appliquéd in place, the design seemed just about perfect, and I couldn't resist photographing it at this stage. Now all I had to do was quilt it and sew on the beads.

Even though it is not tackled until the end, quilting doesn't have to be an afterthought. It can be part of the design process from the very beginning. I do believe that a great quilt is a combination of all of its elements—not just the piecing or just the quilting or just the fabric. I try to keep my mind open as I piece so that when the time comes to quilt, I will be able to tune in quickly to what the quilt needs. Please the quilt first!

Gerber Daisy

Designed and made by Valori Wells; 31" x 31".

✳ MATERIALS

1¼ yards for petals
1¼ yards for background
½ yard for leaves
6" x 6" scrap or ¼ yard for flower center
¾ yard for border and binding
1 yard backing
35" x 35" batting
Beads for the center (optional)

✳ CUTTING

Photocopy patterns A through O (pages 84–88), enlarging as indicated. Trace the patterns and alignment dots on the dull side of freezer paper, and cut out for templates. Cut the petal fabric into four 18" x 22" pieces. Layer the four pieces right side up. Place templates A through G on top, dull side up, and press lightly with a warm iron to adhere. Cut around each template through all four layers of the fabric. Do not unstack. Repeat to cut four each of pieces H through L from the background fabric.

For the flower center, cut one M.

For the leaves, cut one N and one O, adding ¼" seam allowance all around.

For the border, cut four 3½" x 36" strips.

✳ INSTRUCTIONS

1. Mark fabric pieces A through L one stack at a time. At each alignment dot, push a straight pin through all four layers of fabric. Turn the stack over and use a pencil to mark a dot where each pin emerges. Carefully remove the marked fabric. Mark and remove the next piece. Continue until all four pieces are marked. Keep the marked stacks labeled and in order.

Insert a pin at each dot.

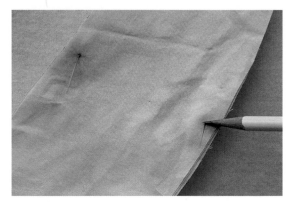

Mark the fabric on the underside.

2. Referring to the diagram below, pin A to B, right sides together. Match the dots precisely along the common edges, then make ⅛" clips to provide ease along any concave sections. Stitch, using a ¼" seam allowance, from the base of the petal to the last dot. Stop.

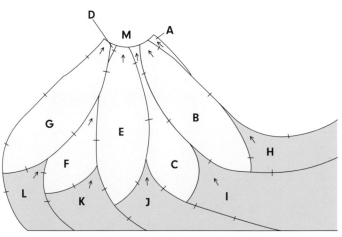

Diagram showing one-quarter of the Gerber daisy.

3. Pin H to AB, right sides together and dots matching. Stitch together, making sure the raw edges are matching at all times. Sometimes it is helpful to use a pin to coax wandering fabric back into position. Set aside the ABH piece without pressing it. (Pressing will be done after the four quadrants are assembled and joined together.)

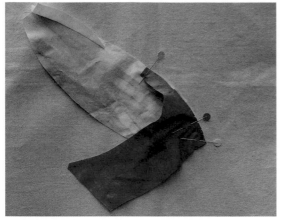
Pin H to AB.

4. Stitch C to I, using the same curved seam piecing technique from steps 2 and 3 and placing the concave I edge on top. Place the CI unit on the ABH unit, right sides together and the concave CI edge on top. Match the dots and pin accurately along the entire edge, folding the seam allowances toward the darker fabric as you come to them. Stitch slowly, making sure the edges match, to ensure a beautifully curved seam.

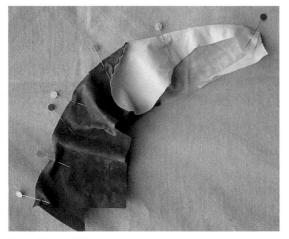
Join CI to ABH.

5. Stitch D to E at the base of the petal. Although D is a little piece, it is not difficult to put in. Stitch J to DE along the outer petal edge.

6. Pin the DEJ unit to the CI edge of the assembled piece, right sides together and matching the dots. In this S-curved seam, the concave edge changes sides. Follow the fabric's lead when placing the pins and stitching. Stitch up to, but not over, the seam allowance between E and J. Remove the work from the sewing machine.

Sew S-curved edges in sections.

7. Flip it over to reveal the other concave edge. Push the seam allowance aside as you stitch the remainder of the seam.

8. Stitch F to K; then add L. Join the FKL unit to the EJ edge of the assembled piece.

9. Join G to the DEFL edge of the assembled piece. Pin and stitch this S seam as in steps 6 and 7. This completes one-quarter of the Gerber daisy.

One-quarter of the Gerber daisy.

10. Repeat steps 2–9 to make four quarters. Stitch the quarters together, joining the ABH and GL edges. Press, first on the wrong side and then on the right side. Square up the quilt top to 25" × 25".

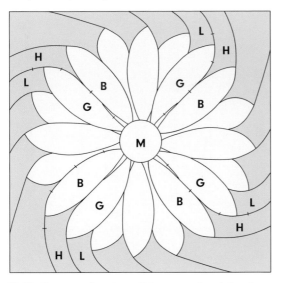

Quilt diagram showing all four quarters joined.

11. Pin a border strip to each edge of the quilt top, right sides together and with the excess border fabric extending evenly at either end. Stitch ¼" from the edge, starting and stopping ¼" from the corner of the quilt top. Press the seam allowance toward the border.

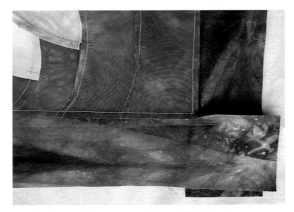

Stitch the border strips to the quilt top.

12. To miter the corners, lay the quilt on a flat pressing surface, right side up. Overlap the border strips at one corner. Fold under the top strip at a 45° angle so it meets the edge of the adjoining border strip. Pin. Press the fold.

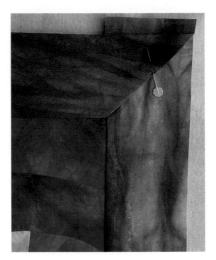

Fold, pin, and press the miter.

13. Remove the pin. Fold the quilt diagonally, right side in, so that the borders lay on top of each other with the edges matching. Pin. Beginning at the inside corner of the quilt, stitch on the fold line toward the outer edge. Trim the excess fabric to ¼", and press the seam open. Repeat for the other three corners.

14. Needleturn-appliqué the flower center M and the leaves to the quilt top. Fold under a small section of the edge to be appliquéd, finger-pressing to give the fabric a little memory. Bring the needle up from the back of the fabric, and catch one or two threads on the underside of the fold. Insert the needle directly down through the background fabric and pull through to the wrong side, so that the stitch is concealed. Continue stitching around the appliqué shape about ³⁄₁₆" at a time, using the point of the needle to turn under the raw edge of the appliqué as you go.

Needleturn Appliqué

15. Layer and finish the quilt. I started by outlining all the shapes. I stitched closely spaced lines in the petals from the center out, stitched veins in the leaves, and did outline quilting in the background. I hand-sewed beads to the flower center (see close-up on page 79).

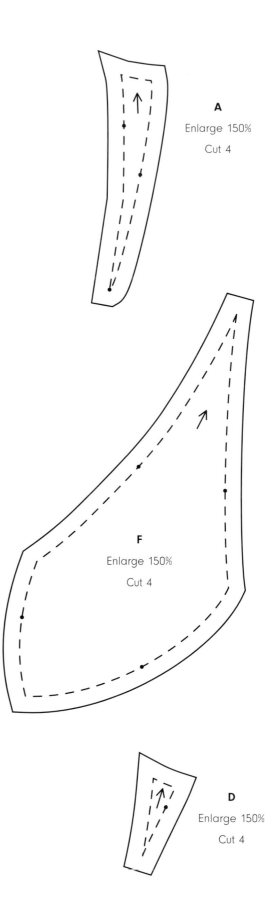

A
Enlarge 150%
Cut 4

F
Enlarge 150%
Cut 4

D
Enlarge 150%
Cut 4

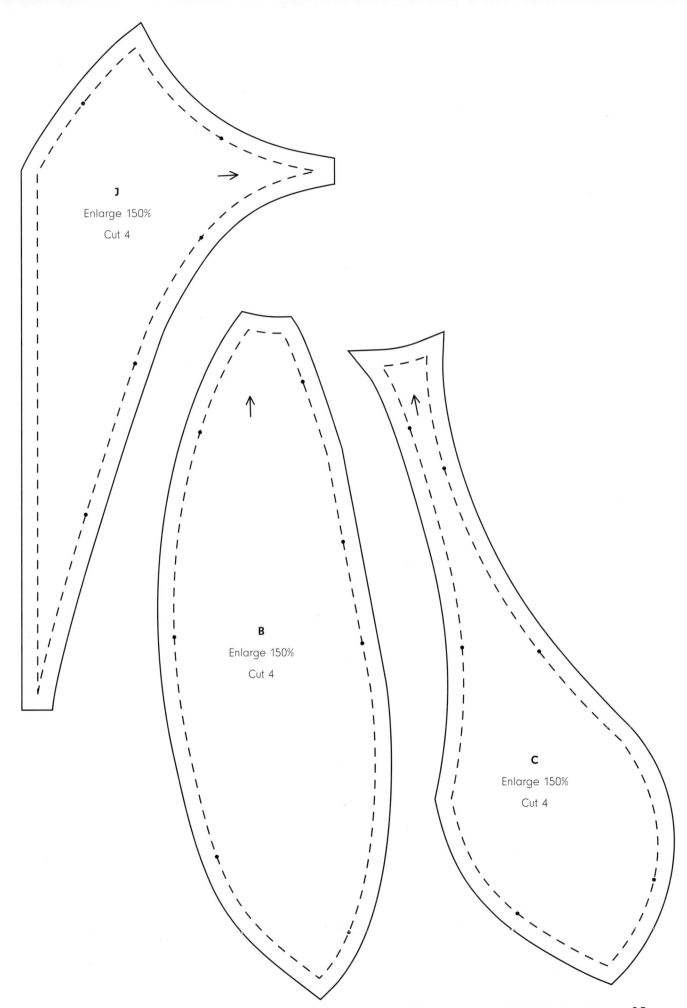

J

Enlarge 150%

Cut 4

B

Enlarge 150%

Cut 4

C

Enlarge 150%

Cut 4

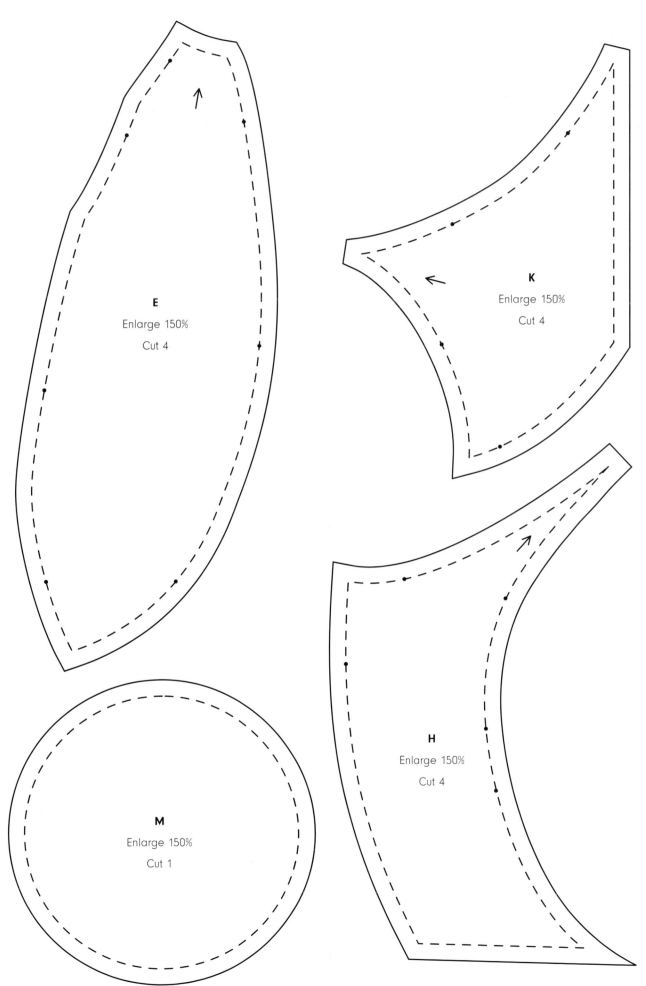

E

Enlarge 150%

Cut 4

K

Enlarge 150%

Cut 4

H

Enlarge 150%

Cut 4

M

Enlarge 150%

Cut 1

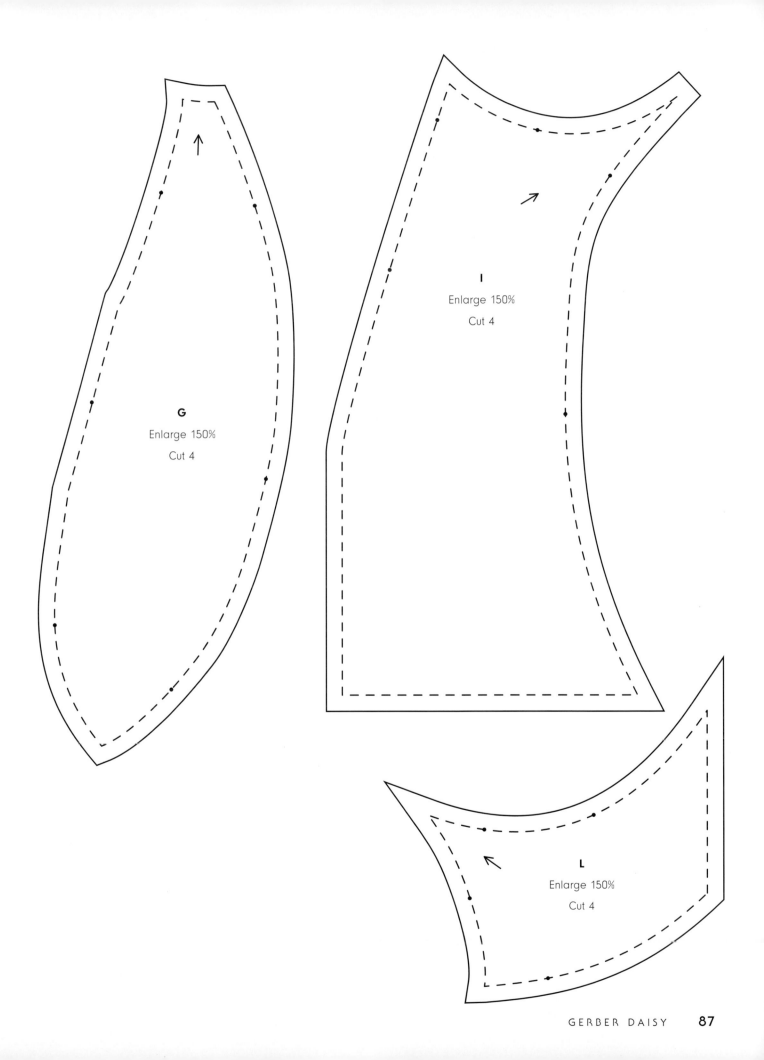

G

Enlarge 150%

Cut 4

I

Enlarge 150%

Cut 4

L

Enlarge 150%

Cut 4

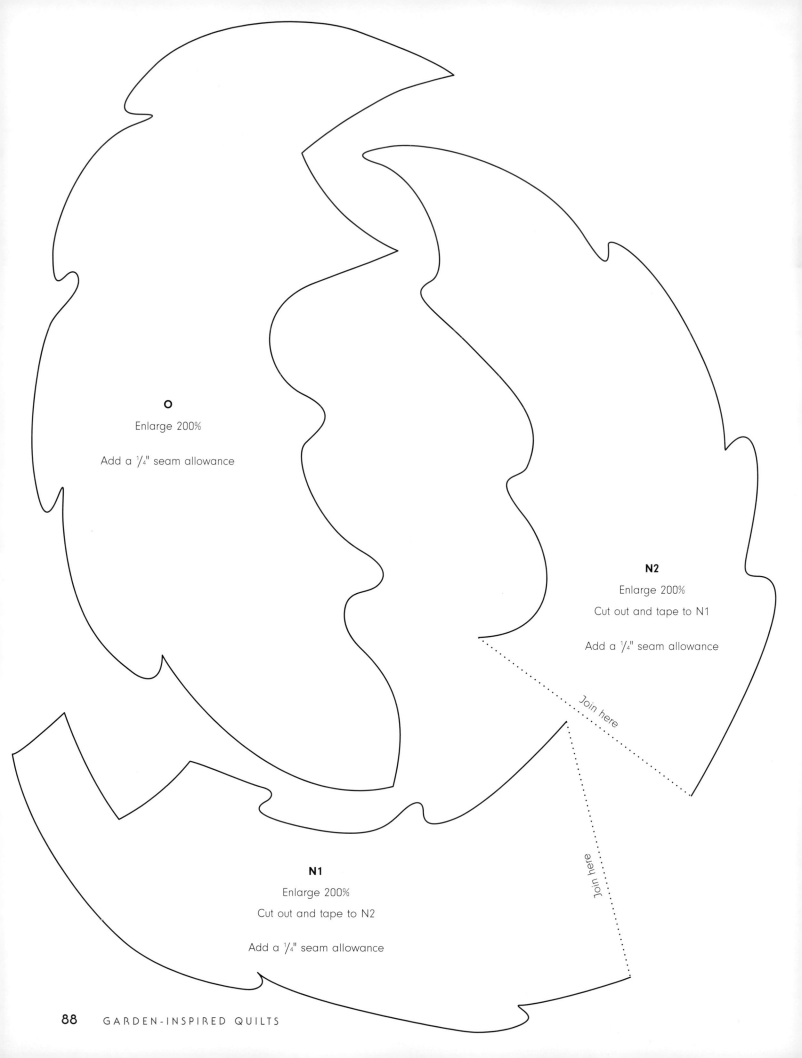

O

Enlarge 200%

Add a ¹/₄" seam allowance

N2

Enlarge 200%

Cut out and tape to N1

Add a ¹/₄" seam allowance

Join here

Join here

N1

Enlarge 200%

Cut out and tape to N2

Add a ¹/₄" seam allowance

Kenmar Farm Baskets

BY SALLY FREY

I have known Jean and Valori for some years and was very excited to know they were coming to photograph my garden and interview me for their book. Our visit was an eye-opening experience for me in many ways. After walking around the yard and taking notes, Valori loaded her camera and started setting up. It took her a while to set up for each shot, to get the right angle and distance—things I never thought much about before, being a point-and-shoot photographer myself. Jean carried the equipment, and we talked quietly in the background, Jean explaining what Valori was seeing and trying to capture on film.

Watching Valori work inspired me to start taking more photographs. Once she explained the "reference shots" concept to me, I realized that I had a garden full of ideas. Reference photos don't have to be picture-perfect in the sense of appearing in a book or magazine. Rather, they serve as a reminder of different colors and shapes. They can also capture the mood created by a particular setting, the time of day, or weather conditions. Little scenes created within the frame of the camera lens could even become quilts within themselves. Using photography to trigger the memory gave me a new way of enhancing my quiltmaking.

During their visit, Valori and Jean were very taken with a 1930s basket quilt that I acquired several years ago. It happened to be on the bed where Jean was to sleep. They wanted to photograph it in the garden, so the next morning we took it outside and put it on an old green swing that is mounted on a tree in the front yard. And of course my cat Snickers had to crawl onto the quilt where he likes to nap.

As Jean and I visited, she related a story to me about her quilt *Tossed Salad* from *Through the Garden Gate*. She told me how she actually took her fabric into the vegetable garden to audition it for the quilt. I never thought of doing that! When I was making *Kenmar Farm Baskets*, I decided to give it a try and took the batiks out to the garden. I wanted to match up my fabrics to the cottage-style flowers planted around the bench. I found auditioning this way very helpful, especially with the lavenders.

It was Jean who suggested I make a "new" version of the basket quilt. The property where our farmhouse is built was previously a chicken farm belonging to Ken and Martha Gilson. The street in front of the house is called Kenmar after them, and that's how I came up with the name "Kenmar Farm Baskets." I knew I wanted the quilt to have a folk art feeling. What makes the antique quilt unusual is the large size of the baskets and their arrangement on the quilt surface. The secret to obtaining such close basket spacing is appliqué.

Plaids are some of my favorite fabrics to work with, and I liked the idea of using plaid textures to create baskets. I collected many more plaids than I actually needed to ensure that I'd have plenty of choices. It's easier for me to eliminate a fabric that is not going to work than to find one more fabric that will. Once the plaids were chosen, I paired each one up with a different batik. It was at this point that I gathered up my fabrics in a basket and made that auditioning trip out to the garden. If it had been a time of year that the flowers weren't in bloom, I could have looked at my reference photographs.

Once the baskets were made, I worked on arranging them on the background fabric. I had chosen a subtle plaid with barely visible lines that made perfect informal guidelines for placing the appliqués. Sandy Globus, the owner of Ocean Wave Quilts, told me a quick way to piece the background in three panels, instead of two, so that I didn't have a seam running down the middle. By placing the baskets unusually close together, fiddling with the color placement, and giving each handle its own distinct bend, I was able to mimic the folk art look I had admired in antique quilts.

The lettering across the top was an afterthought. When I had all the baskets stitched in place and viewed the quilt from a distance, I didn't care for the boxy shape. I felt the quilt needed to be longer. Adding a new panel with the quilt name spelled out in letter appliqués was my solution.

Pam Clark did the machine quilting. I requested flowers inside the handles of the baskets, and when I got the quilt back, I was thrilled. It looks like the baskets are filled with wildflowers that are spilling out all over the quilt. The Jeans Stitch variegated embroidery thread created an English cottage garden look just like the little vignette in my yard. This seemed only fitting, since it was the garden that inspired those colors in the first place.

Kenmar Farm Baskets

Pieced and appliquéd by Sally Frey; machine-quilted by Pam Clark; 90" x 98½".

⬚ MATERIALS

5 yards for baskets background

1/8 yard each of twenty different
   plaids

1 fat quarter (18" x 22") each of
   twenty different batiks (coordinate
   each batik to a plaid)

1 1/2 yards for letters background

5/8 yard plaid for the appliqué letters

1 1/4 yards for borders and sashing

8 yards backing

94" x 103" batting

Monofilament thread for machine
   appliqué (optional)

Jeans Stitch variegated embroidery
   thread (optional)

⬚ CUTTING

For each basket (20 total), do the
following:

Cut a batik into an 18" square. Fold
   diagonally, place a ruler on the
   fold, and cut 1" from the fold. Set
   aside the resulting 2"-wide bias
   strip for the basket handle.

From the remaining batik, cut six
   3 7/8" squares; then cut diagonally
   into half-square triangles for the
   basket body and base.

From a plaid fabric, cut eight 3 7/8"
   squares; then cut diagonally into
   half-square triangles for the basket
   body and setting triangles.

For the baskets background, cut the
   fabric in half, for two 2 1/2-yard
   lengths. Place right sides together.
   Trim off the selvages; then stitch
   the trimmed edges together on
   both sides. Cut through one layer
   only straight down the middle,
   parallel to the stitching lines.

Open out, press the seams, and
trim to 84 1/2" x 74". Turn so the
seams run horizontally.

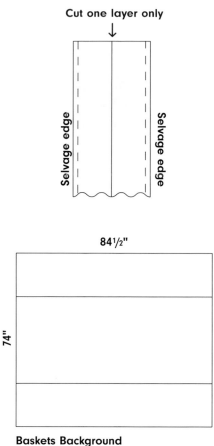

Baskets Background

For the letters background, cut and
   piece the fabric to make an 84 1/2"
   x 17" panel.

For the borders, cut ten 3 1/4"-wide
   strips. Piece together end to end,
   and cut two 3 1/4" x 90" strips for
   the top and bottom borders and
   two 3 1/4" x 93" strips for the side
   borders.

For the sashing, cut three 3"-wide strips.
   Piece together end to end, and cut
   one 3" x 84 1/2" strip for the sashing
   between the two backgrounds.

⬚ INSTRUCTIONS

1. Stitch ten plaid and ten batik
half-square triangles together in
pairs. Press toward the plaid. Trim to
3 1/2" square.

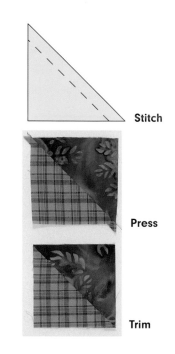

2. Arrange the ten pieced squares
in a triangular shape as shown. Fill
out the rows with single plaid triangles. Stitch together in rows; then
join the rows (Row 1 to Row 2, etc.).

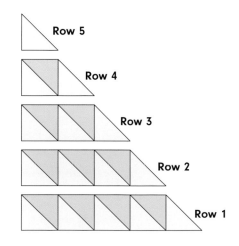

The basket is assembled by joining the rows and adding two batik triangles for the base.

3. Place one batik base triangle on the basket as shown, with the bottom of the triangle extending ³/₈" below the edge of the basket. Stitch to within ¹/₄" of the top edge of the triangle (the allowance will be pressed under later). Add the second base triangle in the same manner.

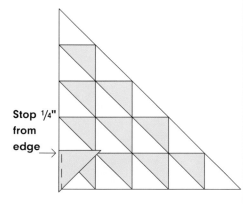

Stop ¹/₄" from edge →

4. Repeat steps 1–3 to make 20 baskets total. Press the raw edges of each basket ¹/₄" to the wrong side all around.

5. Lay each handle strip facedown on the ironing board. Fold and press the long raw edges to the middle to make a 1"-wide bias strip. Shape the strip into a curve, steam-pressing as you go, to fit the pieced basket. Each handle will be unique, and quirky curves will add to the character of your quilt.

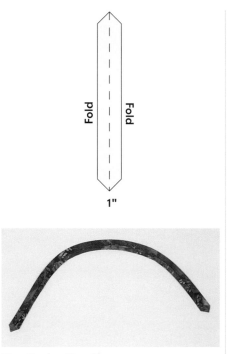

Fold   Fold

1"

Bias Basket Handle

6. Arrange the baskets on the quilt top, spacing them as shown in the photo (page 93). Make a note of your color placement. Pin-baste three baskets in place, including the bias handle, and remove the others. Using monofilament thread, blind-stitch the baskets in place by machine. Pin a few more baskets to the quilt top and repeat, continuing until all the baskets are stitched down.

7. Decide on a name or short message for the top of your quilt. Hand-draw the letters you will need, or use a computer to type and print them in the font of your choice. Enlarge the letters on a photocopier to approximately 7" tall. Cut out. Use the templates to mark and cut the letter appliqués from fabric, adding ¹/₄" all around. Press under the ¹/₄" allowance. Arrange and appliqué

the letters to the background panel as you did the baskets.

8. Stitch the sashing strip to the top of the appliquéd basket background. Add the lettered background panel. Press. Add the side borders and press. Add the top and bottom borders. Press.

9. Layer and finish the quilt. Pam Clark used Jeans Stitch variegated embroidery thread to machine-quilt flowers around the baskets and in the area under handles. The baskets are quilted in a scroll design.

Quilting Designs

Enlarge to desired size

Quilting Designs

Enlarge to desired size

Solitude

BY VALORI WELLS

Solitude was influenced by a combination of things: Mom's quilt *Summer Celebration*, my love of butterflies and flowers, and my desire to make a quilt that appeared "larger than life."

I saw *Summer Celebration* develop before my eyes. Mom created her dragonfly and leaves from realistic images but then used the fabric and thread to give the quilt a playful, stylized look. I watched as the quilt found its own path through the various color and design trials that Mom went through. Her work gave me a unique opportunity to see the creative process up close and in action. I envisioned doing something similar with a butterfly as my subject.

I have always loved butterflies, particularly their delicacy as they dance from flower to flower. Their fluttery movements make them rather tricky to photograph,

however—a challenge to my patience. I felt myself shying away from a realistic interpretation that would have to be perfect in form and design, opting for more creative freedom. I studied my photographs and pictures in a book on butterflies to gather ideas for the angle and view. It would be easier to do a side view than a frontal where both sides matched. As I was leafing through my photographs, I came across an image of a metal butterfly ornament set against a pretty green ground cover. This photo provided just the inspiration I needed to make the jump from realistic to a more stylized interpretation.

Before I could start picking fabric, I needed to find a flower for my butterfly to rest on. When I photograph flowers, I try to capture a variety of angles—underneath, on top, and from different sides.

Sometimes I have the chance to photograph a single plant in stages from bud to full flower. These images make perfect design references—even if I never make a quilt with that particular Gloriosa daisy.

Coneflowers and echinacea have always intrigued me. I like the way the center protrudes, exposing itself, while the petals flow down from the base like a skirt. My only dilemma was the color. I didn't want pink, white, or yellow in my quilt. I had one photograph of a rust coneflower, but that color didn't do it for me either. I figured that my flower, like my butterfly, needed to go beyond reality. I decided on the vibrant red of a zinnia or poppy.

The next question up was how to translate the flower shape into fabric. I knew appliqué was the best way to capture the shape of the drooping petals, but I didn't want to cut them all from one piece of fabric. That's when I remembered Mom's zinnia petals and how she stitched and flipped different fabrics to muslin to create lines and subtle color changes. This became the technique I would use, too.

I chose gold fabric for the very center of the flower, to suggest pollen. Visualizing pointy shapes for the rest of the center, I drafted a semicircular base with points. By stitching two identical shapes together and turning it right side out, I eliminated the step of turning under all those raw edges. Next I made smaller single points to slip under the center piece. Layering the pieces lent a three-dimensional aspect, precisely the textured effect I was after.

It is always interesting to me how ideas emerge from simple, subtle influences that I may not have noticed before. How did I know to chose a coneflower for my butterfly? Another flower would have had me redesigning the petals, pushing them aside, but this flower, with its downward-growing petals, already made the perfect butterfly landing pad.

When my first collection of batik fabrics arrived at the store, I found myself gravitating toward the multicolored sunflower print. Its gold and purple tones made it the perfect fabric for the butterfly wing. I could overlay black bias tape to make the scrolled design and fill in the remaining details later with quilting. The butterfly body needed to be dark but not black. A midnight blue fabric fit well but was a little boring. Since this piece

was small, I decided to let it be until I had the rest of the quilt figured out. I also left the antennae until the end so that I could play with the color. The background color was a given: green, nature's neutral. It was just a matter of picking the right green, something that would work with the other colors in the quilt without competing with them. I based my leaves on a variety of photographs, shaping them to suit my whim and cutting them from hand-dyed lime green fabric. I didn't give any thought to making the leaves true to nature; my focus was on giving the flower a little personality. Developing the leaf design across the lower part of the quilt let me counterbalance the empty space in the top left corner. I must admit I wasn't too thrilled with the quilt up to this point, but I wasn't worried. Intuitively, I knew a border in the right color would spark the design. I decided to try

a fabric that would pick up the purple tones in the butter-fly wing. I worked in some of the same wing fabric as an inset border. Once I had the border pieces in place, the transformation was amazing. The quilt came alive. It seems that no matter how much I try to plan a quilt to the very end, there are always unexpected elements, and this border was one of them. Transforming moments like these make quilting exciting for me and more than make up for the times I get discouraged.

When I finally sat down to quilt—a task I truly love and look forward to—I was a little overwhelmed. I started off on the flower center, quilting spiky lines to mimic the dimensional texture captured by my camera lens. Gaining confidence, I moved to the petals and the leaves. This was fun. I quilted veins in both leaves with dark thread, which

showed up nicely against the light fabric. Next, I went to the butterfly wing. The bias tape swirls provided a predetermined design that was easy to follow. I played with two different ideas on other areas of the wing and ended up pulling out the quilting that didn't work. Removing those stitches wasn't much fun, but it was important for me to try both ideas. The background presented a challenge in that there was already a print in the fabric that I didn't want to compete with. I chose an unobtrusive green thread and stitched long blades of grass that grew up out of the bottom of the quilt and became incorporated into the design. I kept the border simple by repeating the swirl design from the wings in purple thread. As excited as I was about starting the quilting, I still got stuck and had to work through the creative process to find the best results.

Solitude

Designed and made by Valori Wells; 51½" x 84½".

■ MATERIALS

2¼ yards background*

½ yard each of four reds for coneflower petals

2 yards muslin to foundation-piece the petals

1 yard green for stem and leaves

1 yard for butterfly wing

¼ yard for butterfly body

⅓ yard for antennae and body accents

¼ yard gold for flower center

⅓ yard brown for flower center detailing

¼ yard for border insert

1 yard for border

½ yard for binding

11 yards ¼"-wide prefolded black fusible bias tape (used in making stained glass quilts)

3¾ yards backing

55" x 87" batting

Decorative machine embroidery threads

*The background fabric purchased for this quilt was 45" wide. If your fabric is narrower, adjust the quilt dimensions slightly to compensate.

■ CUTTING

Enlarge patterns A through S (pages 105–107) 400% on a photocopier and cut out. To use the patterns, pin them to the appropriate fabric at least ½" apart. Cut out each piece ¼" beyond the pattern edges all around.

For the petal foundations, cut one each of A through I from muslin.

For the stem and leaves, cut one each of J, K, and L from green fabric.

For the flower center, cut one M from gold fabric and six N, six O, six P, and two Q from brown fabric.

For the butterfly, cut one each of R1, R2, and R3 for the wing, and one S for the body. Cut two 1" x 16" bias strips for the antennae and one 1" x 12" bias strip for the body accents.

For the background, cut a 44½" x 77½" piece.

For the border insert, cut seven 1" x 42" strips. Piece the strips end to end, and cut two 1" x 44½" strips for the top and bottom inserts and two 1" x 77½" strips for the side inserts.

For the border, cut seven 4" x 42" strips. Piece the strips end to end and cut two 4" x 44½" strips for the top and bottom borders and two 4" x 84½" strips for the side borders.

■ INSTRUCTIONS

1. Begin the foundation piecing with muslin petal A. Cut a long strip of red fabric, and place it right side up on the muslin foundation. Cut a second strip in a slightly different shade of red. Place it facedown on the first strip, matching the raw edges to be joined. Machine-stitch through all the layers ⅛" to ¼" from the raw edges. Flip the second strip over and press. Cut and stitch a third strip to fill out the remainder of the petal foundation, if needed. Trim the excess red fabric even with the muslin edge all around. Repeat to foundation-piece petals B through I, cutting and stitching the red fabrics one piece at a time. Vary the values and place the strips at different angles to create a shadowy effect, as shown in the quilt photo at left.

2. Place the brown pieces N through Q right sides together in pairs. Machine-stitch ¼" from the edge all around. Trim all the points. On piece Q, clip at each V almost to the stitching. Cut a slit in each piece through one layer of fabric only. Turn right side out through the opening and press flat.

3. Test-fit pieces A through Q on the background fabric, and mark their positions. Hand-baste the leaves, stem, and nine red coneflower petals in place. To needleturn-appliqué the pieces, fold under a small section of the edge, finger-pressing to give the fabric a little memory. Bring the needle up from the back of the fabric, and catch one or two threads on the underside of the fold. Insert the needle directly down through the background fabric and pull through to the wrong side, so that the stitch is concealed. Continue stitching around the appliqué shape about ³⁄₁₆" at a time, using the point of the needle to turn under the raw edge of the appliqué as you go. Clip the inside curves as you come to them so the appliqué lies flat. Be sure to choose a thread

color that matches the appliqué fabric to camouflage the stitches.

Needleturn Appliqué

4. To complete the flower center, needleturn-appliqué M. Next, tack down the nine pods, overlapping them at the base for a textured look. Appliqué piece Q last.

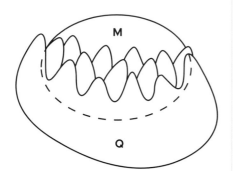

5. For the butterfly wing, join pieces R1, R2, and R3, making ¼" seams. Press. Position the wing on the quilt and pin in place. Run the black tape along the swirl lines, starting at the inside of the swirl and pinning as you go; tuck in and conceal the raw cut ends. Press to fuse in place and set the curves. Run the tape around the edges of the wing in the same way, concealing the raw edges. Fuse in place. Secure by topstitching.

6. For the antennae, press the bias strips in half lengthwise, wrong side in; then press a gentle curve in each strip. Position each strip as shown in the quilt photo, being sure to place one end so that it will be concealed by the head later. Stitch down ⅛" from the raw edge. Fold each strip back on itself, concealing the raw edge. Fold in the two ends opposite the head. Sew down the folded edges by hand.

7. For the body accent stripes, press the bias strip as in step 6. Cut into thirds. Sew the strips to the body in parallel lines, using the step 6 antennae technique. Needleturn-appliqué the body to the quilt top. The ends of the trim will be turned under as you go.

8. Fold each border insert in half lengthwise, wrong side in, and press. Pin the border inserts to the edges of the quilt, matching the raw edges and overlapping at the corners. Stitch the top and bottom borders to the quilt, catching the inserts in the seams. Press the seams toward the border, letting the inserts face toward the quilt center. Add the side borders in the same manner.

9. Layer and finish the quilt.

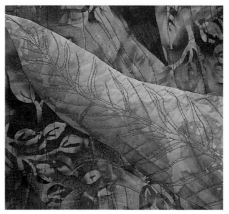

Quilting Details

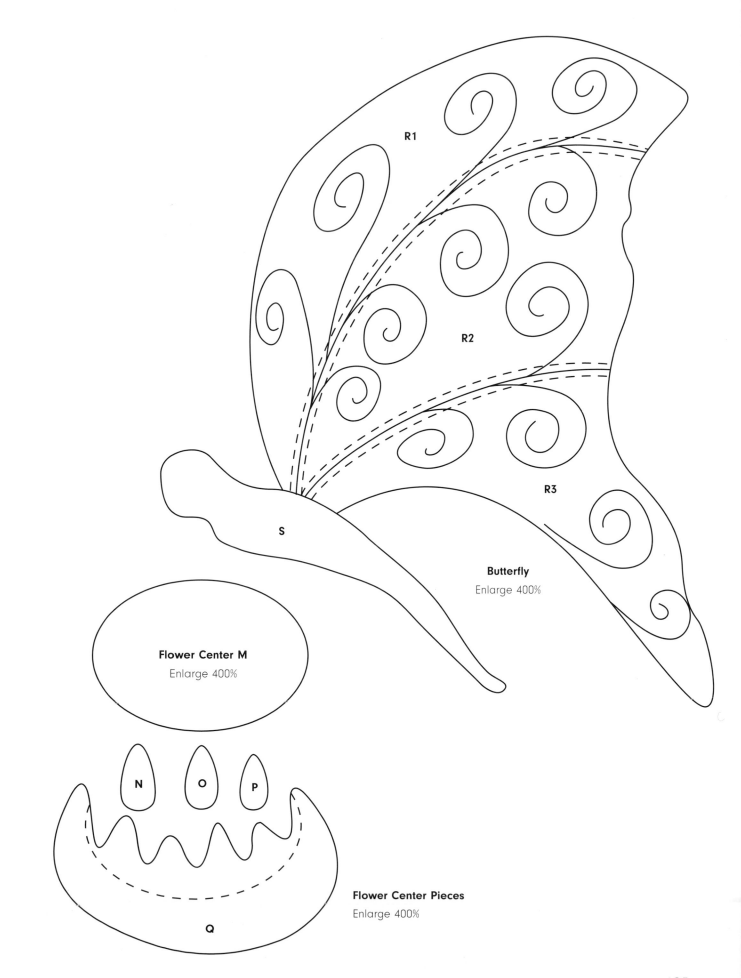

R1

R2

R3

S

Butterfly
Enlarge 400%

Flower Center M
Enlarge 400%

N **O** **P**

Flower Center Pieces
Enlarge 400%

Q

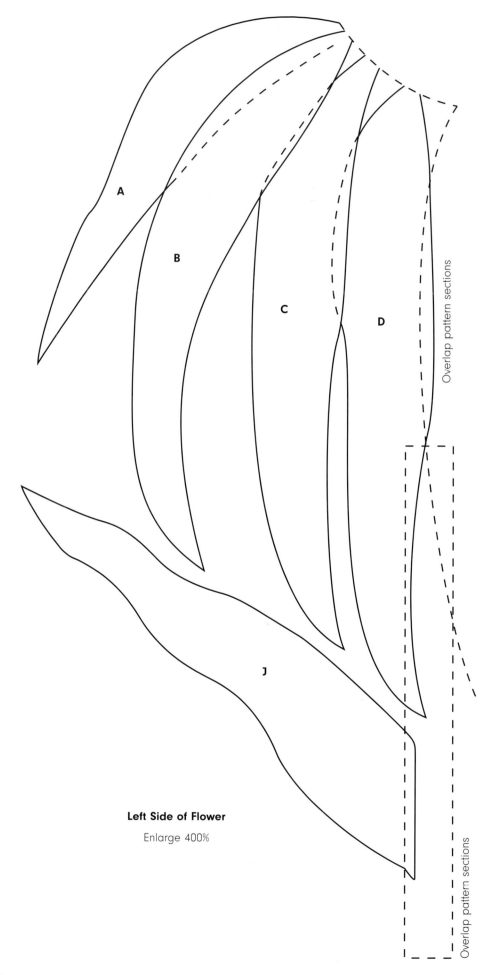

A

B

C

D

J

Overlap pattern sections

Overlap pattern sections

Left Side of Flower

Enlarge 400%

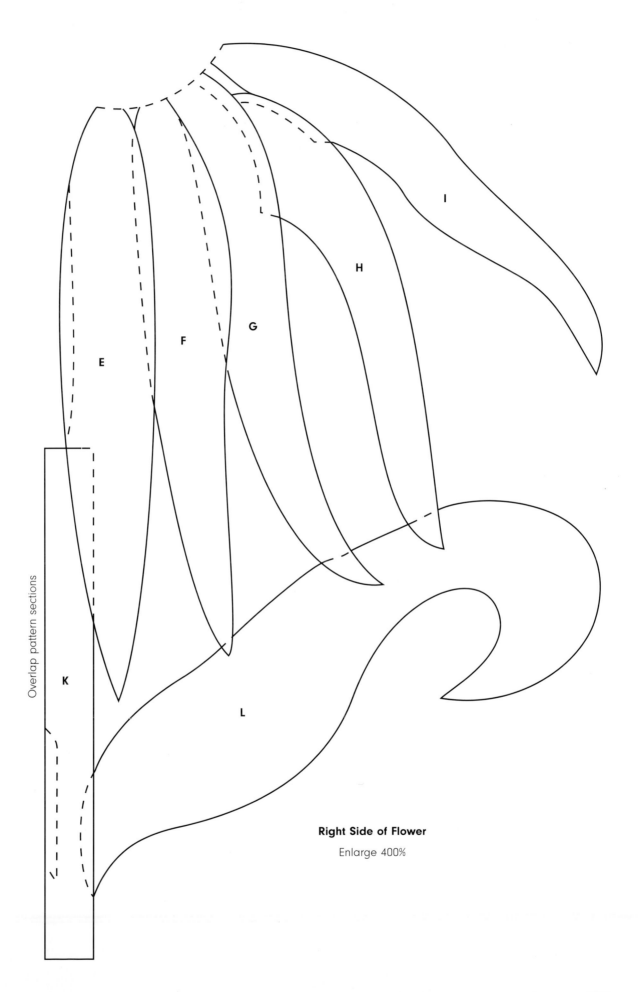

Overlap pattern sections

E

F

G

H

I

K

L

Right Side of Flower

Enlarge 400%

Summer Celebration

BY JEAN WELLS

Having been a quilting instructor for over twenty-five years, I find it enlightening to change hats now and then and become a student. That is why, every couple of years, I take a workshop from someone whose work I admire. Jane Sassaman is one such person. She came to Oregon a few summers ago, and I was fortunate enough to find a seat in her five-day seminar.

Our town's outdoor quilt show had just ended the week before, so I didn't have as much time to think about Jane's workshop and prepare as I would have liked. The topic was designing from nature. On the morning of the first class, I hurriedly picked some of my favorite flowers from the garden—wild lupine, Queen Anne's lace, coreopsis, lavender, wild daisies—put them in a purple antique glass container that had belonged to my grandmother, and off I drove.

I could hardly wait for class to begin. Jane has a wonderful, gentle way of positioning you to discover things for yourself. For two full days, I found myself busy exploring my theme using only tracing paper and a pencil. I was continually surprised by how many new shapes and designs I was seeing in that simple vase of flowers. Although I had been cultivating these flowers in my garden for years, I was drawn to them in a new way.

The lupine leaves in particular fascinated me. They protrude from the stem in a circular manner, and I enjoyed playing with this shape on paper. Then I focused in on one leaf and proceeded to study it intently. As the hours slipped by, I became totally absorbed in leaf vein patterns, sketching and interpreting everything I observed. In Summer Celebration you can see the culmination of this exercise, where the different vein patterns come to life with fabric and thread.

Other plant forms also attracted my attention. The purple lupine flower grows in dense, upright spikes, and it was only through close observation of an individual petal that I became aware of the round ball shape. Several garden photos that I had brought to class showed a plant form that curved up from the ground and circled at the top—perhaps it was a young fern slowly unfurling its frond. In my drawings, I began to see this intriguing shape fitting in with the leaves and growing up directly from the garden floor.

I also had a photograph of a dragonfly. That summer, my garden had become a haven for dragonflies. I could sit outside in my chair and watch dozens of these beautiful creatures darting in and out among the flowers. Studying their bodies and wings became my passion. All kinds of patterns emerged. My next step was obvious: to simplify the dragonfly shape. When I looked closely at the wings, the shapes started resembling simple leaves or flower petals. I began visualizing all kinds of designs for the interior that I could bring to life with fanciful embellishment. I doodled and came up with a variety of patterns, thoroughly enjoying this imaginative activity.

With Jane's encouragement, I started playing with all of these ideas to see how I might incorporate them into a quilt design. This is where I get anxious in the design process. Intuitively, I know this phase is natural and essential, that I am looking for direction, and that direction comes in different forms. Sometimes, more observation is necessary, since clues abound in nature. Other times, taking a mental break is the only way to make a breakthrough. That's when I take a walk or go do the laundry and tell myself I'll see everything with fresh eyes in the morning.

Jane could have solved it for me, but then it would have been her design. Instead, she asked questions and threw out comments to keep me thinking—comments like "tighten up the design," "try more circles," "play with more designs in the dragonfly wings." The next morning, I arrived in class fresh and rested, and the design resolved itself with me as director. Perhaps the best thing I learned in Jane's workshop is to keep trying out new variations. I can't use all of them in one quilt, but now I have all of those new ideas to work from in the future.

Once I nailed down the design, it was time to determine the size of the quilt and enlarge the patterns on a copy machine. I knew I wanted the dragonfly and all its marvelous detailing to appear larger than life. I also wanted the dragonfly to appear in among the leaves, just as it would be in nature. *Summer Celebration* ended up being a large wall quilt.

Two and a half days had gone by, and I had not so much as touched the fabric in my basket. I could hardly believe it. Usually I am not very secure in the design process unless I am touching the fabric. It was a stretch for me to work two days straight with only paper and pencil, but I found the experience invaluable.

When I began pulling out possible fabrics for the dragonfly and leaves, I seemed to gravitate toward bright, summerlike prints. I began envisioning a darker-value background to showcase the more vibrant greens I had chosen for the leaves. After a few rejects, I turned up a deep dark green batik with little chevrons that seemed to work. Those lighter green chevron lines created enough of a pattern that the fabric didn't read as a solid, even from a several feet away.

Now I was into the fun part for me, working with the fabric palette. I love the auditioning and decision making involved at this stage and just keep trying out fabrics until I get the look I want. The combination of fabrics in the wings set the tone for what was needed in the body, and I was hoping a few orange and grape embellishments in the leaf area would pull the eye around the quilt. I find a reducing glass invaluable when it comes to choosing a palette.

What a special workshop this was for me. I left the five-day class with my idea set and most of my fabrics chosen. Jane was quietly encouraging, saying just enough to get me to keep exploring my ideas until I found the right fit on my own. I've never been a big fan of orange and was reluctant to use it, but I realize now that those tiny touches of orange make the design sing.

Jane's demonstration of machine appliqué opened up more creative possibilities for me. It had been years since I had machine-appliquéd, and I now saw with fresh eyes how stitching could create subtle design lines and add detailing. For the first time, I experimented with heavier threads like Jeans Stitch thread for embellishment lines. All those veining details that I had spent hours poring over came to life as I ran the leaves through my sewing machine, adding one stitching line after another. Never before had I let machine appliqué influence the actual design, and I have Jane to thank for introducing me to this approach.

I always question whether a border is needed, but the answer here was clear. The question was, what color? The deep red shades in the dragonfly tail provided the inspiration. I found some hand-dyed red fabric on my shelf with random shading similar to the feeling created in the dragonfly wings. I cut out different strips, playing with the placement to capture the nuances.

Quilting for me is the icing on the cake. To create a unified whole, I look for elements in the quilt design that I can repeat in the stitching. The scrolled lines in the orange tendrils were an obvious motif, and I worked them over the surface of the quilt. On the border, I followed the gently curving lines in the fabric design and worked off these to fill in. I was almost sad to see this quilt finished. I loved working on it and making all of the decisions and doing the stitching.

Summer Celebration

Designed and made by Jean Wells; 48½" x 62½".

▧ MATERIALS

1³/₄ yards for background

1 yard for border insert, wings, and tendrils (I used orange)

1 yard for border, binding, and lower body (I used hand-dyed red)

1¹/₂ yards total for leaves (I used a variety of greens, including hand-dyed greens, to create light and dark interest)

¹/₂ yard total for head and upper body and circles (I used hand-dyed purple)

¹/₃ yard each of two different printed textures for the upper and lower wings (I used orange and purple)

¹/₂ yard total of a variety of printed textures for embellishing the wings (I used greens, yellows, purples, and oranges)

4 yards lightweight fusible interfacing

2 yards paper-backed fusible web

3 yards lightweight tear-away stabilizer

3 yards backing

53" x 67" batting

Embroidery floss to match the tendril and circle fabrics

Coordinating threads for machine appliqué and quilting

▧ CUTTING

Enlarge appliqué patterns A through J (pages 117–119) as indicated.

For the background, cut a piece 42¹/₂" x 56¹/₂".

For the border insert, cut five strips 1¹/₂" x 42". Piece the strips together end to end, and then cut two 1¹/₂" x 42¹/₂" strips for the top and bottom and two 1¹/₂" x 56¹/₂" strips for the sides.

For the border, cut six strips 3¹/₂" x 42". Piece the strips together end to end, and then cut two 3¹/₂" x 42¹/₂" strips for the top and bottom and two 3¹/₂" x 62¹/₂" strips for the sides.

For the leaf appliqués, trace pattern A once and pattern B nineteen times onto lightweight fusible interfacing. Cut the leaves apart, and fuse them to the various greens, referring to the quilt photo (page 113) and close-up (page 115) for color ideas. Cut out the leaves on the marked outlines.

For the tendrils, trace pattern C once, pattern D three times (reverse one), and pattern E twice onto paper-backed fusible web. Allow extra room at the bottom to extend the stems later. Set aside.

For the dragonfly appliqués, trace patterns F, G, H, and I onto lightweight fusible interfacing. Cut the pieces apart, and fuse them to your selected fabrics, referring to the quilt photo (page 113) and close-ups (page 116) for color ideas. Cut out all the pieces on the marked outlines.

For the circles, trace pattern J eight times onto paper-backed fusible web. Cut the circles apart and fuse them to the various purples. Cut out on the marked outlines.

Set aside the remaining fabrics and paper-backed fusible web for the embellishment appliqués, to be made later.

▧ INSTRUCTIONS

1. Embellish the twenty leaves, using both machine embroidery and fabric fusing to make the leaf veins. See page 115 for design ideas. To stitch leaf veins that gradually broaden out, I start with the stitch width set at narrow and then turn the dial to a wider stitch as I sew. Refer to the satin stitch instructions in your sewing machine manual to see how you might create the same effect. Try different thread colors, and be sure to use a lightweight tear-away stabilizer underneath. To make leaf vein appliqués from fabric, draw a wavy vein onto paper-backed fusible web, fuse it to fabric, and then carefully cut it out and fuse it to the leaf. Change the vein lines slightly and vary the fabric combinations so that no two leaves are alike. Use this same fusing technique to give some leaves two background colors, and then alternate the vein colors that go on top of them.

Appliqué and Stitching Designs for Leaf Embellishment

2. Arrange the leaves on the background fabric, over-lapping them as shown in the quilt photo (page 113) and diagram (below). Once your arrangement is set, pin in place. Decide where to position the tendrils, and extend the stems of the tendrils that are marked on the paper-backed fusible web accordingly. Complete the tendril appliqués, and fuse them to the background, hiding the ends under the leaves.

3. Set your machine to a basting stitch. Stitch around each leaf as close to the edge as possible, using tear-away stabilizer on the underside of the background fabric. Turn the quilt to the wrong side. Trim away the background fabric under each leaf about $1/4$" inside the machine basting line to eliminate the extra thickness. Set the machine to a satin stitch, and go around each leaf again to conceal the basting.

Leaf Embellishment Close-up

Quilt Diagram

4. Repeat the stitching and appliqué techniques from step 1 to embellish the dragonfly's wings, body, and head. To prepare the appliqués, trace the interior shapes on patterns F, G, H, and I onto paper-backed fusible web and fuse to your selected fabrics, referring to the quilt photo (page 113) and close-ups (page 111 and below) for color ideas.

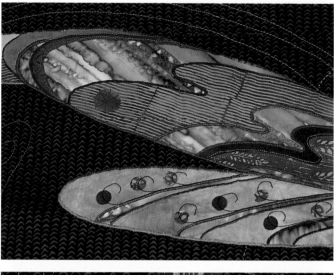

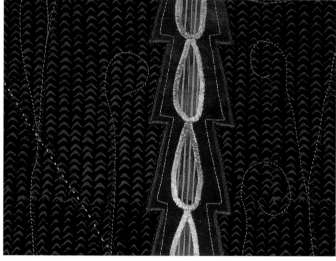

Dragonfly Close-ups

5. Arrange the various dragonfly parts on the background and pin in place. Repeat the technique from step 3 to machine-appliqué the pieces and remove the excess background fabric from behind them.

6. Fuse the circles in place among the leaves. Work buttonhole stitch around each circle and along the edges of the tendrils by hand. Embroider the antennae in stem stitch.

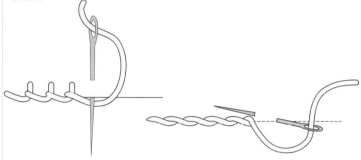

Buttonhole Stitch   **Stem Stitch**

7. Fold each border insert in half lengthwise and press. Pin the border inserts to the edges of the quilt, matching the raw edges and overlapping at the corners. Stitch the top and bottom borders to the quilt, catching the inserts in the seams. Press the seams toward the border, letting the inserts face toward the quilt center. Add the side borders in the same manner.

8. Layer and finish the quilt. I took my quilting ideas from the images on the quilt. First, I outlined the individual leaves, the dragonfly, and the tendrils. I repeated the tendril shapes in the background. I also hand-quilted a large tendril behind the dragonfly, using two strands of orange embroidery floss to make it stand out. In the border, I echoed the lines that appear in the hand-dyed fabric.

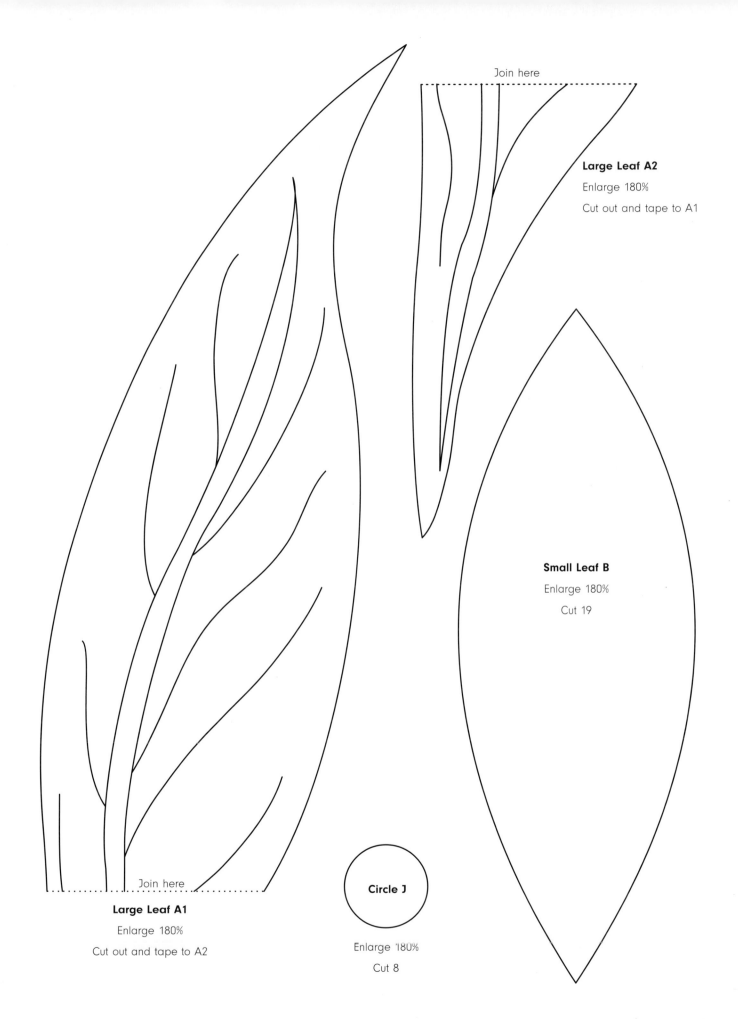

Join here

Large Leaf A2

Enlarge 180%

Cut out and tape to A1

Small Leaf B

Enlarge 180%

Cut 19

Join here

Large Leaf A1

Enlarge 180%

Cut out and tape to A2

Circle J

Enlarge 180%

Cut 8

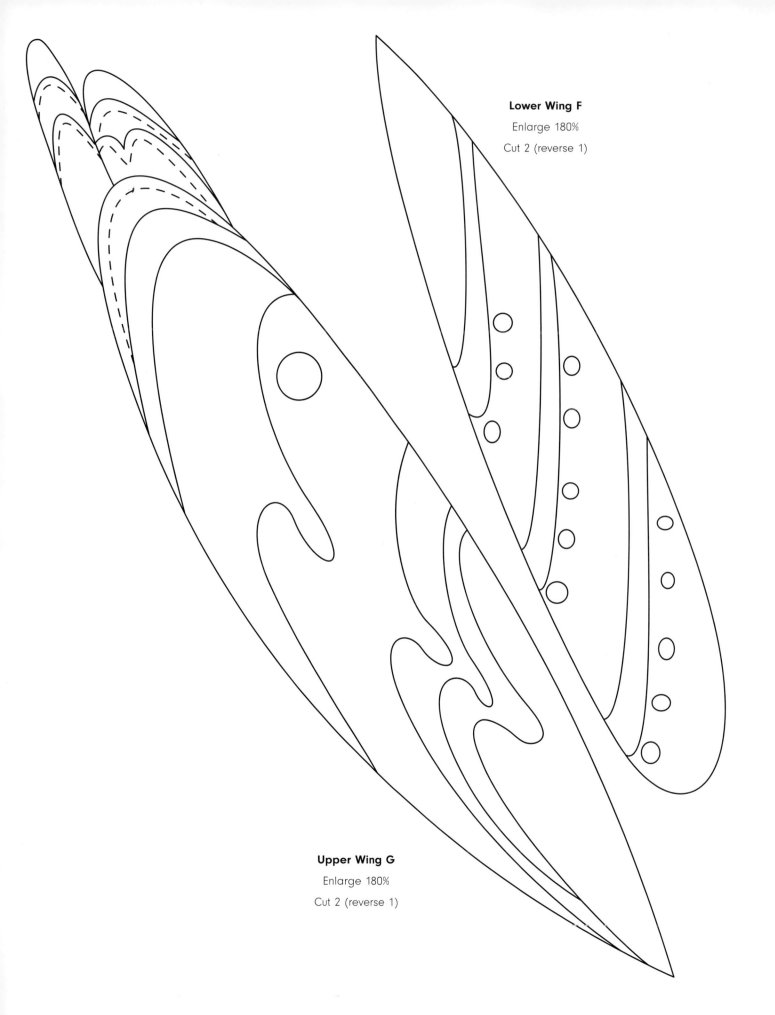

Lower Wing F

Enlarge 180%

Cut 2 (reverse 1)

Upper Wing G

Enlarge 180%

Cut 2 (reverse 1)

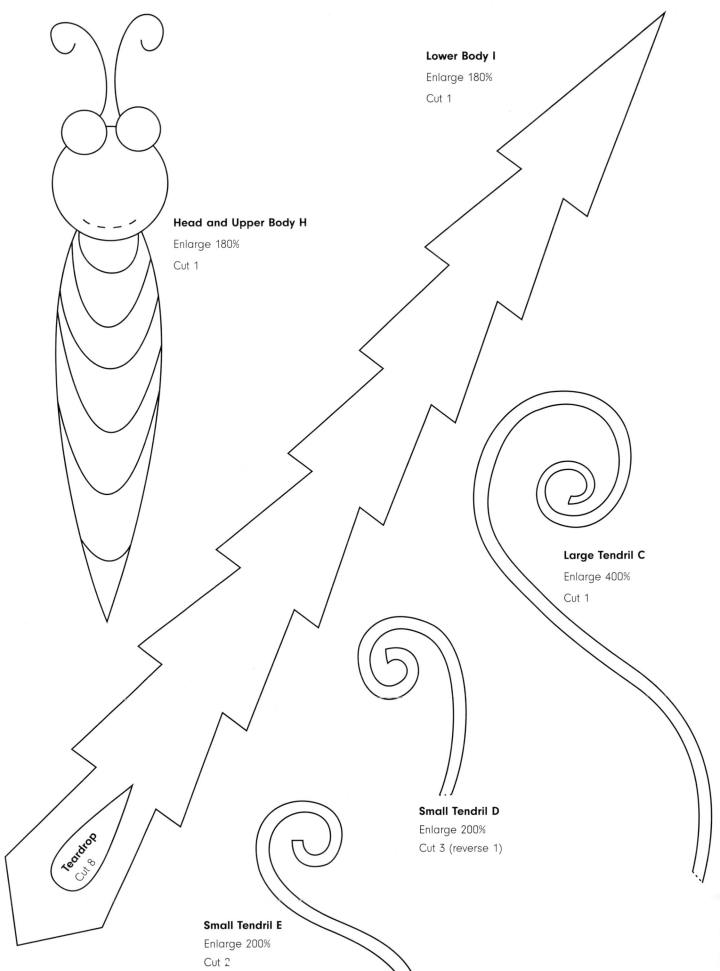

Lower Body I

Enlarge 180%

Cut 1

Head and Upper Body H

Enlarge 180%

Cut 1

Large Tendril C

Enlarge 400%

Cut 1

Small Tendril D

Enlarge 200%

Cut 3 (reverse 1)

Teardrop
Cut 8

Small Tendril E

Enlarge 200%

Cut 2

Zinnias
BY JEAN WELLS

When I was making my quilt *Paradise in the Garden*, I focused on the zinnias' rich colors and their density of growth in the flower bed. With *Zinnias*, I was after a different effect. I wanted to somehow convey the zinnia's characteristic petals. My first stop was the garden, to study the originals.

I love the opportunity gardening gives me to observe while working quietly, undisturbed, in nature. Surrounded by overwhelming beauty, I can pause to take in individual patterns, shapes, and colors. Some zinnias, I found, sported just one round of longer petals. Others, with their multiple layers of smaller petals, struck me as tight little buttons. Petals with upward-curling side edges created exquisitely delicate textures. Compact pistils emerging at the centers reminded me of French knots in embroidery. Another discovery was a miniature five-petal shape that formed a ring at the flower center. The variety in the detailing was mind-boggling.

As is always the case when I am developing a design, my well of ideas had reached a saturation point, and it became necessary to simplify. There was only so much detail I could convey in fabric. The challenge was to find the best expression possible using the fabric medium.

One of my early intuitions about this quilt was that seeing the flowers large, "in your face" so to speak, would make a good statement. I tentatively set up a Nine-Patch grid and penciled in flower colors that I felt best represented the zinnias. Now it was on to the individual flower design. I picked a photograph, placed tracing paper on the top, and traced the shape of the flower. The tracing paper acted as a filter, blurring the detail of the photograph. It literally forced my hand to simplify the design. Tracing also helped me memorize the shape in my mind and silently prepared me for the work ahead.

At this point, I started thinking about how I might sew the emerging design. It does no good to create a shape if I cannot also come up with an effective way to translate it into fabric. My drawing had assumed the shape of a circle with petal lines radiating from the center. My idea was to use these segments to convey details I had observed in the garden. I flirted briefly with the idea of appliquéing the petal layers, but then I decided to try the "stitch 'n flip" approach from Valori's book of the same name.

First, I traced a simple petal shape onto muslin and cut it out. Pulling fabrics from one color family, I cut strips and stitched and flip-pieced a petal. My next step was to determine if I could successfully needleturn-appliqué this shape onto a background fabric. As it turned out, it was very easy and I liked the effect. With the muslin foundation, there were two layers to turn, which created a raised effect that made the flower more lifelike.

I took my simple drawing to the copy center and enlarged it to fit the seventeen-inch block size I was planning. I absolutely loved it large! I came home and made a block. It was perfect. For the flower centers, I chose a tightly packed zinnia print fabric that Valori had designed from our last book, *Through the Garden Gate*. The detail in this fabric generated the same vitality I had seen in the garden flowers. After making a few of these blocks, I got the idea to try a double ring of petals. Back to the drawing board to trace another flower and enlarge it.

I proceeded to make more colored flowers. For each one, I picked a fabric that closely matched the color of the flower and then backed off a tad in each direction, picking both a lighter version and one a touch darker. Some flowers have only three fabrics because that was all I could find. In others, there are five or six. Fabrics with subtle color and texture changes helped me convey the complexity of the flowers with a minimum of stitching. Once again, I took my clues from the garden.

I continued to visualize my giant zinnias in a Nine-Patch arrangement, and when I had nine of them made, I put them up on the design wall in order to choose the sashing. I auditioned more fabrics than I could count, but nothing grabbed me. Something was missing. In need of inspiration, I decided to leave the quilt alone and headed out to the garden.

As I was gazing out over the flower bed, things began to click. The missing ingredient, I realized, was the color excitement generated by the flower bed as a whole. Although each flower is beautiful in itself, they make a more dramatic showing when viewed together. Valori's zinnia fabric offered potential in this direction, so I started experimenting. The fabric looked okay cut into sashing strips, but the effect was still not what I wanted. Sometime over the next couple of days, I got the idea to cut along the flower outlines instead of in a straight line. It worked! Then I went back to the Nine-Patch grid idea and decided on a hand-dyed fabric for the sashing that reminded me of a wood box. The raw edge of the flower fabric was buttonhole-stitched in place.

I wasn't finished yet. Even though I had used greens for the background, it became obvious once the top was pieced that leaves were needed. I designed two-tone leaves, piecing them together on a gentle curve, much as they appear in nature. By inserting a piece of flannel between the leaves and the backing to raise them slightly, they gained dimension.

Little did I know when I started this quilt how it would end up—there was always an element of surprise. "Growing" a quilt is much like planting a seed in the garden and nurturing it into a mature plant. It is a process I truly love.

Zinnias

Designed and made by Jean Wells; 63" x 63".

MATERIALS

⅛ yard each of at least three different fabrics for each
  of the nine flowers (choose different values of the
  same hue for each set)

9 fat quarters (18" x 22") in a variety of greens for the
  background in the blocks

1¾ yards for sashing, borders, and binding

2½ yards muslin for foundation piecing

1½ yards floral for block borders and flower centers

1 yard each of two green fabrics for leaves

1 yard flannel to insert in the leaves

4 yards paper-backed fusible web

3¾ yards backing

67" x 67" batting

Embroidery floss in yellow and to match block borders
  (2 skeins required for borders)

Template plastic

CUTTING

For the blocks, cut nine 17½" squares from the green fat
  quarters.

For the floral borders on the blocks, fuse the paper-
  backed fusible web to the back of about 1 yard of floral fabric. Cut 36 strips 17½" long and approximately
  1½" wide, making one edge straight and the other
  edge following the floral pattern.

Set aside the remainder of the floral fabric for the
  flower centers.

For the sashing, cut six 2½" x 42" strips. From three
  strips, cut six 2½" x 17½" pieces for the vertical sashing. Piece the remaining strips end to end, and cut
  two 2½" x 55½" strips for the horizontal sashing.

For the borders, cut six 4¼" x 42" strips. Piece together
  end to end, and cut two 4¼" x 55½" strips for the
  sides and two 4¼" x 63" strips for the top and bottom.

For the leaves, trace *Paradise in the Garden* patterns D
and E (page 140) onto template plastic; also trace the
full leaf outline. Cut out all three templates. Cut a total
of 23 D and 23 E pieces, adding ¼" seam allowance
all around. Reverse the colors and flip the templates
over for some pairs. Set aside the remaining leaf fabric
and template.

INSTRUCTIONS

1. Enlarge zinnia patterns A and B (pages 130–131)
175%. Trace each petal individually onto template plastic,
and add ¼" seam allowance all around. Cut out on the
outside line. Label each template (A1, A2, etc.). Also make
templates for the flower centers A and B, adding ¼"
seam allowance.

2. Place the petal templates on muslin, and trace
around the edges with a pencil to make muslin foundations for piecing. Make enough muslins for seven A zinnias and two B zinnias.

3. Begin the foundation piecing with petal A1. Cut a strip
of petal fabric 1" to 1½" wide and at least ¼" longer than
the foundation muslin. Place the strip right side up on the
muslin (a). Cut a second strip in a slightly different shade.
Place it facedown on the first strip, matching the raw edges
to be joined. Machine-stitch through all the layers ⅛" to ¼"
in from the raw edges (b). Flip the second strip over and
press (c). Continue to stitch and flip new strips until the
muslin foundation is completely covered. Trim off the excess
fabric even with the muslin edge (d). Repeat until the petals
for seven A zinnias and two B zinnias are completed.

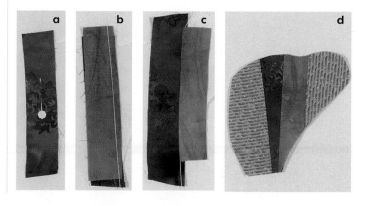

4. Lay a green background block face up on a flat surface. Arrange petals A1 through A12 in a ring on the block. Pin in place.

5. Needleturn-appliqué the outer edge of each petal, starting with A1 and proceeding in numerical order around the flower until you reach the starting point. Turn under the muslin as well as the flower fabric $1/8"$ to $1/4"$ to create a raised edge on the petals, finger-pressing to give the fabric a little memory. Bring the needle up from the back of the fabric, and catch one or two threads on the underside of the fold. Insert the needle directly down through the background fabric and pull through to the wrong side, so that the stitch is concealed. Sometimes I pushed up the edges and tacked them down to add dimension to the petals instead of appliquéing them flat. It is not necessary to appliqué edges that will be concealed by an overlapping petal. Appliqué the petals for seven A zinnias. For each double-ring zinnia, appliqué petals B1 through B11 in the outer ring first, and then appliqué petals B12 through B22 in the inner ring over them.

6. Cut a center for each flower from the floral fabric, using the templates made in step 1. Pin a center to each flower. Needleturn-appliqué the edges, concealing the raw edges of the petals. Embellish each flower center with yellow lazy daisy stitches. Use six strands of embroidery floss in the needle so that the stitches will stand out.

Lazy Daisy Stitch

7. Place four floral border strips on each block, right side up and straight edges matching. At each corner, decide which strip will overlap the other. Trim the top strip to redefine the flower outlines as needed, and cut away the excess bulk. Fuse the border strips in place. Work buttonhole-stitch along the inner border edge using three strands of embroidery floss.

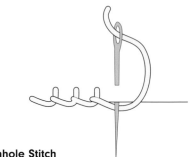

Buttonhole Stitch

8. Referring to the quilt diagram, join the blocks and vertical sashing strips together in rows. Press. Join the rows, adding the horizontal sashing in between. Press. Add the borders. Press.

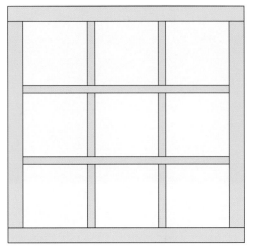

Quilt Diagram

9. Sew the leaf pieces D and E right sides together in pairs, making a $1/4"$ seam. Use the full leaf template to cut 23 leaves from green fabric and 23 leaves from flannel. Place each pieced leaf on a solid leaf, right sides together, and then place on top of a flannel leaf. Stitch together a scant $1/4"$ from the edge all around, leaving a 2" opening for turning. Trim the points and clip the curves. Turn right side out. Press. Hand-sew the opening closed. Topstitch vein lines. Arrange the leaves on the quilt top as shown in the photograph. Tack in place by hand, pushing up on one end for added dimension.

10. Layer and finish the quilt. I outlined the flowers and then echoed this stitching outward. For the petals, I used matching thread to quilt straight lines that radiate from the flower center. In the outer border, I quilted simple leaves.

Zinnia Pillow

18" x 18"

MATERIALS

1¹/₈ yards for background and pillow back

¹/₈ yard of four different monochromatic fabrics for flower

5" x 5" floral for the center

1 yard muslin for flower foundation and pillow top backing

22" x 22" batting

20" x 20" pillow form

Embroidery floss for center

Template plastic

CUTTING

From the background fabric, cut one 19" square for the pillow top and two 12¹/₂" x 19" rectangles for the pillow back.

From the muslin, cut one 19" square.

INSTRUCTIONS

1. Enlarge zinnia pattern A (page 130) 175%. Trace each petal individually onto template plastic, and add ¹/₄" seam allowance all around. Cut out on the outside line. Label each template (A1, A2, etc.). Also make a template for the flower center A, adding ¹/₄" seam allowance.

2. Follow the zinnia quilt instructions, steps 2–3 (page 127), to foundation-piece the twelve petal appliqués.

3. Follow the quilt instructions, steps 4–5 (page 128), to needleturn-appliqué the petals to the pillow top.

4. Follow the quilt instructions, step 6 (page 128), to needleturn-appliqué and embroider the center of the flower.

5. Layer the pillow top, batting, and muslin backing. Machine-quilt through all layers. Trim the batting even with the fabric edge.

6. Press one long edge of each pillow back ¹/₄" to the wrong side; fold in again and topstitch. Overlap the two pillow backs, right side up, as shown. Baste together along the raw edges.

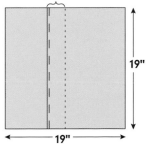

Overlap pillow backs

19"

19"

7. Place the pillow back on the pillow front, right sides together. Stitch ¹/₂" from the edge all around through all layers. Retrim the batting as close to the stitching as possible. Clip the corners, turn right side out, and insert the pillow form from the back. Using a pillow form that is slightly larger than the cover makes for a plumper pillow.

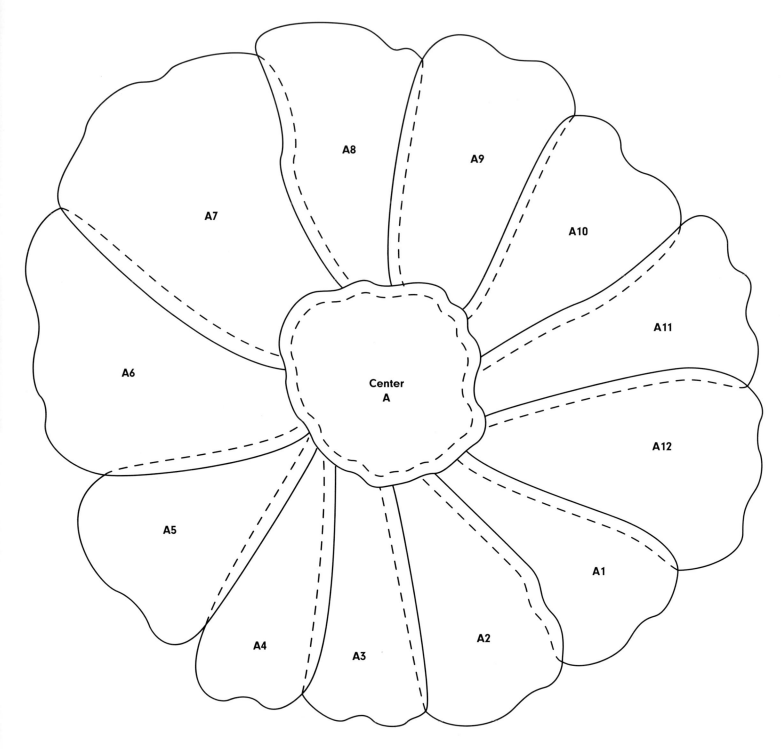

Zinnia A

Enlarge 175%

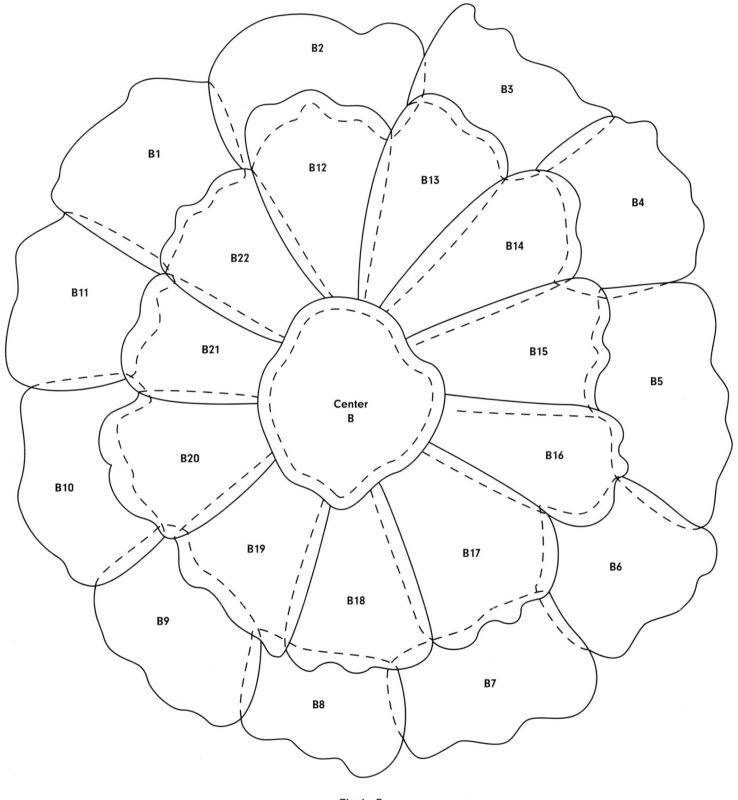

Zinnia B

Enlarge 175%

Paradise in the Garden

BY JEAN WELLS

My flower garden offers constant inspiration for color combinations. The zinnias are especially endearing. In the winter, as I leaf through seed catalogs, I am repeatedly lured by their bright, playful hues.

Here in central Oregon, zinnias must be started indoors from seed because of the late frosts we get being near the mountains. I plant the tiny seeds in mid-April and then anxiously wait for them to germinate and sprout, first one set of leaves and then another. Once the plants are established, I move them outdoors during the day. Eventually, I can leave them outdoors at night as well, covering them to protect them from the evening chill. In mid-June, the big day arrives when I can transplant my young zinnias in well-cultivated garden soil. Most go into their own flower bed, but I put some of the taller ones in the vegetable garden to liven up all the various shades of green.

It takes about a month for the flowers to start blooming. "Cut and Come Again" is one of my favorites. To tell the truth, I think of all zinnias in this way—the more you cut, the more they come again. On warm summer mornings, as I cut and toss zinnias in a basket, one palette after another emerges. These same flowers will show up an hour later in my two stores in Sisters, The Stitchin' Post and The Wild Hare. A gift store with a garden theme, The Wild Hare carries vases of every size and shape. The zinnias from my garden sell a lot of vases.

What I have really noticed, cutting and living with zinnias as closely as I do, are the subtle changes in value. A single color family can yield bright clear orange, red-orange, melon, and apricot. When those same cut zinnias are randomly tossed in a basket, a spontaneous color study unfolds. Capturing the intensity of this color as well as the petals' subtle shading differences became my goal in *Paradise in the Garden*.

I am always amazed how yellows, golds, reds, purples, and oranges all work together. But I am also struck by how the bright, clear, intense values cooperate with softer, more muted shades. The greens in the leaves and stems are important to consider, too, because they act like a neutral, offering the eyes a rest while simultaneously highlighting all the warm colors in the flowers.

To choose a palette for this quilt, I pulled fabrics from my stash and brought them out to the flower beds. Natural light is best for matching up colors, and I found some amazing selections. Once a basic palette was in place, I added fabrics purchased during my teaching trips around the country. I've always enjoyed the time spent traveling, when I am collecting ideas and materials for future quilts. Evidently, the colors of those zinnias in my summer garden were memorized in my mind, because I had no trouble finding more fabric to use.

Color isn't the only secret my zinnias revealed to me. The round, compact shape of the flower, repeated over and over, is a soothing design element. Figuring out a way to represent the zinnias' round shape in the quilt design became paramount in my mind. As I was mulling this over, I was also getting ready to teach a class using Karen Stone's book New York Beauties. It dawned on me that four New York Beauty blocks pushed together would create a large circle. Here was a way I could capture that plump, round aspect of the zinnia that I was so fond of. If I joined four different blocks, the interior would become even more interesting with its competing arcs and points.

Once I started working on the quilt, the new challenge became balancing its many colors. I began by making several blocks, working with a variety of colors. Next, I put them on the design wall in groups of four, to get a feel for the colors and the overall composition. As I made more blocks, I added them to the mix, working from the top down. It was inevitable as the layout progressed that some blocks would change position. I could see that the strong colors like red needed balancing. It would not do to have all the red weighing down one side of the quilt. It seemed that the more blocks I made, the more the decisions made themselves.

Right about here, I hit that spot in the design process when the quilt starts telling me what it needs. In this case, it needed leaves. Photographs that capture the essence of the garden become vital references at times like this, particularly as fall and winter close in. When I look at a photograph, I ask myself, "What am I really seeing? What is it about this picture that I want to express using fabric?" The answers to these questions provide added stimulus to my quilt design. I knew I wanted to capture how these flowers grow in nature, and I started thinking about how I could portray stems and leaves and their rich junglelike texture.

Valori had just finished her book *Stitch 'n Flip*, and that technique, with its random design possibilities, was fresh in my mind. I tried the idea on a sample piece of fabric and was able to create stemlike piecing. I could see that with the addition of leaves the impression would be there.

Once I could visualize the finished quilt, I was able to pull the rest of the design together. I prefer working this way, always leaving the door open for new possibilities rather than planning the entire quilt at the start. I usually end up with a better design. At this end stage, I fine-tune the colors and piecing and focus in on the details to get exactly the look that I want. A narrow pieced border that repeats the flower colors seemed a fitting frame for the flowers and foliage in the interior. The geometry of these colorful rectangles adds another dimension to the quilt. A final border in a deep blue-green frames the design.

To develop a quilting pattern, I reexamined the detailing in the flowers. Since I like the spontaneity of free-motion quilting, I stitched leaves and petal shapes. I highlighted the wedge shapes in the arcs with echo quilting. *Paradise in the Garden* is my interpretation of the zinnias in my garden, but the design could easily be done in other palettes.

Paradise in the Garden

Designed and made by Jean Wells; 76½" x 76½".

MATERIALS

8 yards total of a variety of fabrics for the blocks
  (including greens for the foliage blocks)

1 yard green print for the setting triangles

1/2 yard each of two green fabrics for the leaves

1/2 yard flannel to insert in the leaves

1 3/8 yards good-quality muslin for foundation piecing

1 1/4 yards for outer border and binding

4 3/4 yards backing

81" x 81" batting

CUTTING

For the leaves, trace patterns D and F (page 140) onto
  template plastic; also trace the full leaf outline. Cut out
  all three templates. Cut a total of 13 D and 13 E pieces
  from the two different greens, adding 1/4" seam
  allowance all around. Reverse the colors and flip the
  templates over for some pairs.

From the muslin, cut three 17" squares, one 17 3/8" square,
  and one 12 5/8" square. Cut the 17 3/8" square diagonally
  for the bottom setting triangles. Cut the 12 5/8" square
  diagonally for the bottom corners.

From the green print, cut three 13" squares and one 12 5/8"
  square. Cut the 13" squares into twelve quarter-square
  triangles for the side and top setting triangles. Cut the
  12 5/8" square diagonally for the top corners.

For the inner border, choose nine of the zinnia flower colors. Cut a 2 1/2" x 24" strip of each color and set aside.

For the outer border, cut eight 2 1/2" x 42" strips. Piece the
  strips end to end, and cut two 2 1/2" x 72 1/2" strips for the
  top and bottom and two 2 1/2" x 76 1/2" strips for the sides.

Save the remainder of the fabric for piecing the blocks.

INSTRUCTIONS

1. Photocopy patterns A, B, and C (pages 140–141)
enlarging as indicated. Cut out each one on the outside
cutting lines. You will need to make a new copy of B for
each block sewn.

2. Select the fabrics for A, B, and C. For the best effect,
choose two highly contrasting fabrics for the pieced
arc B. Place patterns A and C on the right side of your
chosen fabrics and cut out. Cut a 5 1/4" x 22" strip from
each of the B fabrics.

3. Set the stitch length of your sewing machine to 18 to
20 stitches per inch. Place the two B strips right sides
together, with the fabric for the larger odd-numbered
wedges, or background, on top. Place pattern B on the
strips, marked side up, as shown. Pin if desired. Stitch on
the solid line between #1 and #2, from one edge of the
paper to the other.

Paradise in the Garden *uses twenty different arc patterns from the book* New York Beauties *by Karen Stone. One of Karen's patterns appears on pages 140–141 for you to try out the technique. The arc is foundation-pieced on paper. The paper is torn off after the arc has been pressed and the excess fabric cut away. If you have never tried this process, you will like the results—sharp points that are accurate.*

If you decide to make Karen's other blocks, set each pattern out and count the number of fabrics. Choose a multicolored print for the top of the block and two fabrics with high contrast to each other for the pieced arc. Secondary arcs and other shapes can be worked in more multicolor prints or novelty fabrics. Stick with solids, prints that read as solids, and hand-dyed fabrics for the pieced arcs, as multicolor prints can lose definition at the points. For more information on New York Beauties, *see page 143.*

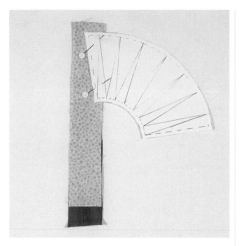

Stitch the first seam from edge to edge.

4. Carefully trim the excess background fabric behind #1 even with the straight edge on the left of the paper pattern. Flip the work over, fold back the point fabric, and finger-press the seam. Fold the paper pattern on the next seam line between #2 and #3, and trim the point fabric $1/4$" beyond this fold line. Finally, trim the top and lower edge of the point fabric even with the curved edges of the pattern.

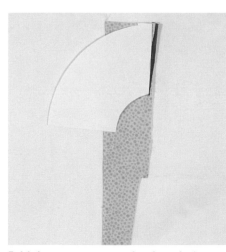

Fold the paper pattern back and trim.

5. Line up the background fabric along the edge of the point fabric, right sides together. Flip the work over so the paper pattern is on top, and stitch the new seam. Flip the work over, fold back the background fabric, and finger-press the seam. Trim away the excess background fabric and prepare to stitch the next seam, as in step 4. Continue repeating steps 4 and 5, alternating the two fabrics, until the arc is completed. Press the arc and trim off the remaining excess fabric even with the paper. Tear off the paper.

Realign the fabrics and stitch the next seam.

6. Make $1/8$" clips at $1/2$" intervals along the inside curve of piece A. Consistent clipping will result in a smooth seam. Fold piece A in half to locate the middle of the curved seam, and mark with a pin. Repeat to mark the outside curved edge of pieced arc B. Place A and B right sides together, matching the pins at the midpoint. Pin through both layers at the midpoint; then remove the marker pins. Line up and pin the straight side edges together also.

Join A to the pieced arc along the outside curve.

7. With the clipped edge on top, machine-stitch along the curve $1/4$" from the edge. Use a pin to help ease the fabric as you go along. Stitch about an inch or so, and then stop and reposition the raw edges. The curve is gentle enough that the process should go smoothly.

8. Repeat steps 6 and 7 to clip the inside curve of B and to join B and C. On the wrong side, press the seams away from the pieced arc. Press again from right side. After pressing, I like to apply a light coat of spray starch to stabilize the block.

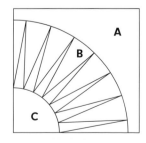

Join C to the pieced arc along the inside curve.

9. Repeat steps 2–8 to make a total of 46 blocks. Try to use fabrics from each color group, but vary their position from block to block, so that the colors move around the quilt. When you've completed several blocks, start putting them up on your design wall or laying them out on a bed. Decide on several new fabric combinations. Cut out the pieces, complete the arcs, then do a few more. You are building a design.

10. To begin a foliage block, place a strip of green fabric on a 17" muslin square diagonally, from corner to corner. The strip should be cut at a slight angle to make a wedge shape. Place a second strip in a slightly different shade of green on the first strip, right sides together. Pin in three places through the two fabrics and the muslin foundation. Stitch through all of the layers $1/4$" from the raw edges of the strips. Flip the second strip over and press.

11. Continue to stitch and flip new green strips to the block, angling them to create wedgelike shapes. Work from the center strip out to each side, letting the raw edges extend beyond the edges of the muslin. When the muslin foundation is covered, press and starch the block. Trim the excess fabric even with the muslin edge.

Foundation-piece green strips for the foliage blocks.

12. Add the completed foliage block and the remaining muslin foundation pieces to the design board. Repeat steps 10 and 11 to fill the remaining muslin pieces with green strips that will run vertically when viewed in the quilt.

13. Add the green setting and corner triangles to the design board, and evaluate the overall layout. Rearrange the blocks until the design is pleasing to you. Sew the blocks and triangles together in diagonal rows, and then join the rows together as shown.

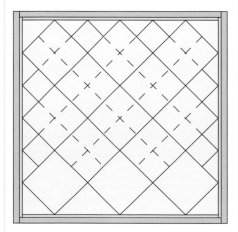

Quilt Diagram

14. Stitch the leaf pieces D and E right sides together in pairs, making a $1/4$" seam. Press each seam toward the darker fabric. Use the full leaf template to cut 13 leaves from flannel. Back each pieced leaf with a flannel leaf, position on the quilt, and hand-baste in place.

15. Turn under the flannel as well as the leaf fabric $1/8$" to $1/4$" to create a raised edge, finger-pressing to give both fabrics a little memory. Bring the needle up from the back of the fabric, and catch one or two threads on the underside of the fold. Insert the needle directly down through the background fabric and pull through to the wrong side, so that the stitch is concealed. Continue stitching around the leaf, about $3/16$" at a time, using the point of the needle to turn under the raw edges as you go. Repeat to needleturn-appliqué each leaf.

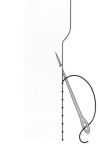

Needleturn Appliqué

16. Arrange the nine zinnia-colored border strips side by side in a pleasing order. Machine-stitch the longer edges together. Press the seams in one direction. Cut across the seams in $1\frac{1}{2}$" segments. Stitch the segments together end to end to make one long strip. From the strip, cut two $70\frac{1}{2}$" strips for the top and bottom inner borders and two $72\frac{1}{2}$" strips for the side inner borders. (You will be cutting through a rectangle.) Add the top and bottom inner borders to the quilt, and then add the side inner borders. Add the outer borders in the same manner.

17. Layer and finish the quilt. I always look for shapes and images in the piecing that can be repeated in the quilting. On this quilt, I found myself working intuitively once I got started. I would work in an arc for a while and then switch to one of the setting triangles or the foliage.

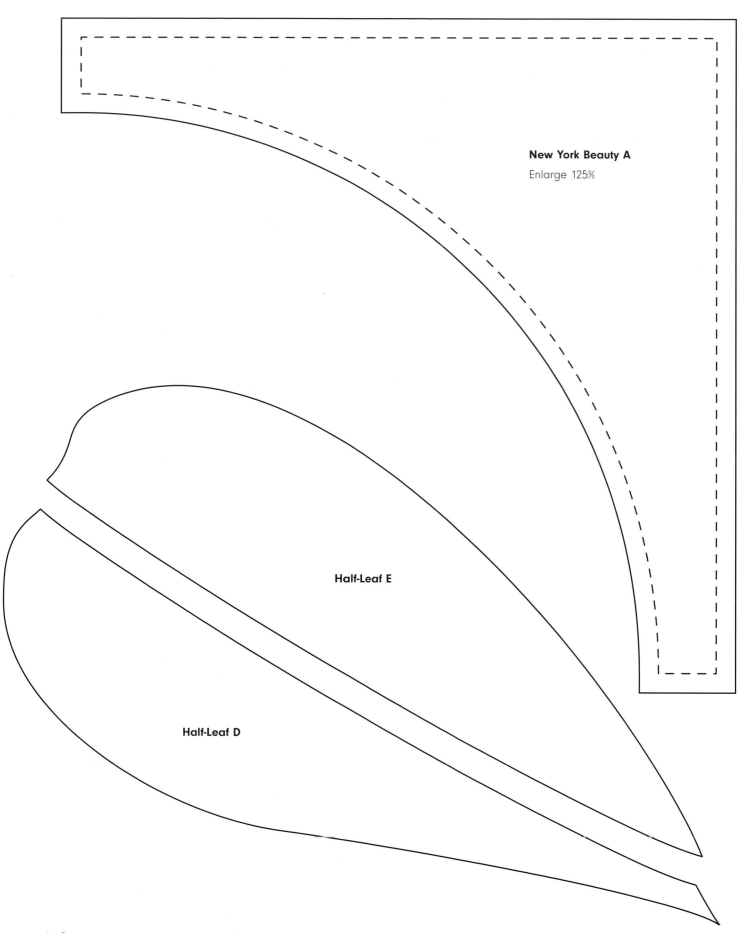

New York Beauty A
Enlarge 125%

Half-Leaf E

Half-Leaf D

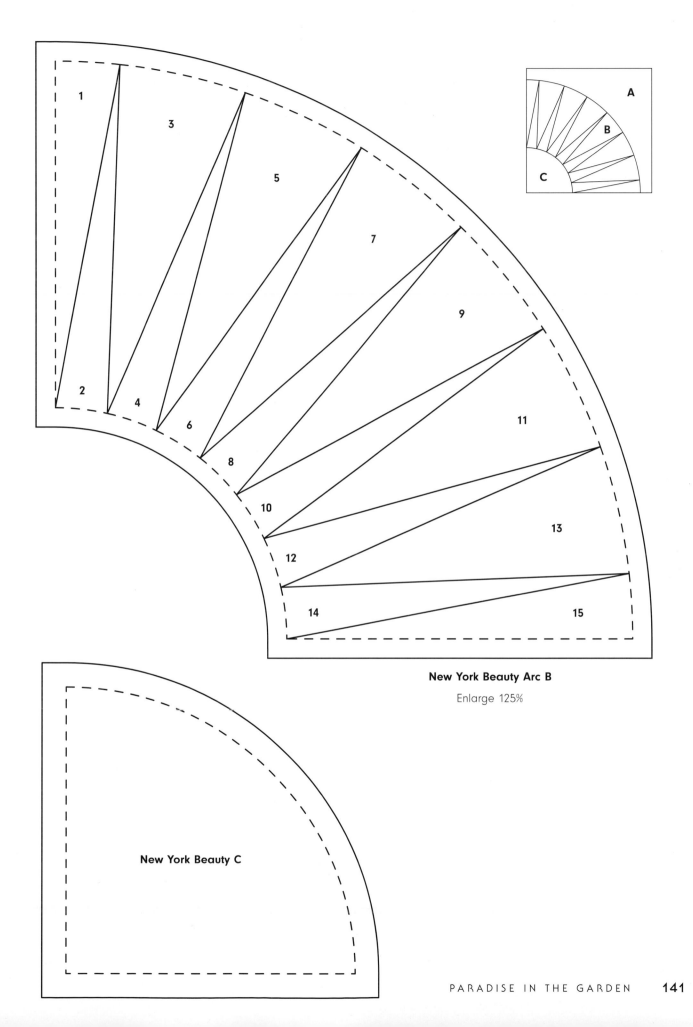

New York Beauty Arc B

Enlarge 125%

New York Beauty C

About the Authors

The combination of quilting, gardening, and photography has become a passion for this mother-daughter team. Valori's talents as a photographer capture nature and the garden at its best, whether it be a close-up, intimate photograph of a wasp on a pine bough or a full field of wildflowers. Through her camera lenses, she takes you on an inspirational journey that translates into quilts. Both members of this team are avid quilters who like to experiment with color and design and to convey the essence of the garden in their quilts.

Valori grew up in a quilting household where she was exposed to the business side as well as the creativity of quilting. She began assisting her mother with quilting ideas at a young age, and her interest eventually blossomed into a career. At Pacific Northwest College of Art, Valori studied her first passion—black and white photography. She received a bachelor's degree in fine art photography and was chosen as the "Outstanding Photographer" in her senior year.

Working together with her mother on their first book, *Everything Flowers*, opened up the world of color photography to her. She is a self-taught color photographer, and her images have been featured in the authors' four subsequent books. Valori's first solo book, *Stitch 'n Flip*, explores an age-old technique in a unique way. Presently, she spends her time designing textiles, photographing gardens, and learning the retail business.

Jean has been sewing since she was nine years old but didn't discover quilting until her twenties when she was teaching home economics. It was love at first sight, and she has been quilting ever since. Twenty-six years ago she opened The Stitchin' Post in Sisters, Oregon, one of the first quilt shops in America. Sharing her love of quilting with others through books, lectures, workshops, and her store brings her much satisfaction. She has appeared on HGTV's *Simply Quilts*, written numerous articles for magazines, and taught business classes and quilting workshops worldwide. In 2000 her business in Sisters, Oregon, received the local "Business of the Year" award. She has also received the Michael Kile Award for Lifetime Achievement in the quilting industry and been inducted into the Primedia Hall of Fame as one of the first "independent retailers."

Jean opened her second retail store, The Wild Hare, several years ago. It is known for its unique garden-related decorative items and creative garden accessories. Gardening and quilting are two special interests that keep her creative juices flowing. In 2000 her quilt *Paradise in the Garden* won the imagination award in the Millennium Quilt Contest. She used the cash prize to build a small greenhouse garden shed that is surrounded with lavender and has a lavender-colored door.

Sources

For Further Reading

The Appliqué Handbook
Becky Goldsmith and Linda Jenkins
Piece O' Cake Designs
2904 E. 27th Street
Tulsa, OK 74114
(918) 746-0408
pieceocake@compuserve.com

*Curves in Motion: Quilt Designs
and Techniques*
Judy B. Dales
C&T Publishing
P.O. Box 1456
Lafayette, CA 94549

New York Beauties
Karen K. Stone
5418 McCommas Blvd.
Dallas, TX 75206-5626
(918) 746-0408

Piecing: Expanding the Basics
Ruth B. McDowell
C&T Publishing
P.O. Box 1456
Lafayette, CA 94549

Quilting Books and Supplies

The Stitchin' Post
P.O. Box 280
311 West Cascade
Sisters, OR 97759
(541) 549-6061
www.stitchinpost.com

Cotton Patch Mail Order
3405 Hall Lane, Dept. CTB
Lafayette, CA 94595
(800) 835-4418
www.quiltusa@yahoo.com

Decorative Garden Accessories and Gifts

The Wild Hare
P.O. Box 280
321 West Cascade
Sisters, OR 97759
(541) 549-6061
www.stitchinpost.com

Bunnies By The Bay
Bloomsbury House
617 East Morris Street
La Conner, WA 98257

Other favorites by Jean & Valori Wells from C&T Publishing:

Everything Flowers
Quilts from the Garden
by Jean & Valori Wells

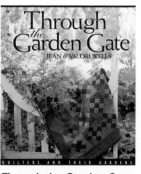

Through the Garden Gate
Quilters and Their Gardens
by Jean & Valori Wells

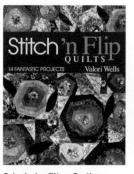

Stitch 'n Flip Quilts
14 Fantastic Projects
by Valori Wells

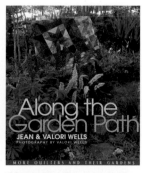

Along the Garden Path
*More Quilters and Their
Gardens*
by Jean & Valori Wells

For more information write
or call for a free catalog:
C&T Publishing, Inc.
P.O. Box 1456
Lafayette, CA 94549
(800) 284-1114
e-mail: ctinfo@ctpub.com
website: www.ctpub.com

Index